Cross-Platform Perl

Cross-Platform Perl

Eric F. Johnson

M&T BOOKS

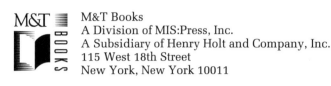

M&T Books
A Division of MIS:Press, Inc.
A Subsidiary of Henry Holt and Company, Inc.
115 West 18th Street
New York, New York 10011

Limits of Liability and Disclaimer of Warranty
The Author and Publisher of this book have used their best efforts in preparing the book and the programs contained in it. These efforts include the development, research, and testing of the theories and programs to determine their effectiveness.

The Author and Publisher make no warranty of any kind, expressed or implied, with regard to these programs or the documentation contained in this book. The Author and Publisher shall not be liable in any event for incidental or consequential damages in connection with, or arising out of, the furnishing, performance, or use of these programs.

All products, names and services are trademarks or registered trademarks of their respective companies.

Printing history:
First edition—1996
Second printing—October, 1997 with minor corrections

Library of Congress Cataloging-in-Publication Data
Johnson, Eric F.
     Cross-platform Perl / by Eric F. Johnson.
          p.   cm.
     ISBN 1-55851-483-X
     1. Perl (Computer program language) 2. World Wide Web servers. 3. Cross-platform software development. I. Title.
     QA76.73.P22J64 1996   96-35498
     005.13'3—dc20   CIP

10 9 8 7 6 5 4 3 2

Associate Publisher: Paul Farrell
Executive Editor: Cary Sullivan
Editor: Laura Lewin
Copy Edit Manager: Shari Chappell
Copy Editor: Sara Black
Technical Editor: Kevin Reichard
Production Editor: Joe McPartland

To Norma, and many years together

Contents

viii

Chapter 2: Perl Basics 33

Chapter 3: Working with Files 77

Contents

x

xi

Chapter 6: Launching Applications...... 153

Chapter 7: Perl Packages and Modules 179

Section II: Advanced Perl 195

Chapter 8: Perl for System Administration 197

Chapter 9: Perl for Web Pages 211

Chapter 10: Perl for Cross-Platform Development 261

xiv

Chapter 11: Perl for Client-Server 279

Chapter 12: Graphical Interfaces with Perl and Tk.......................... 297

Appendix A: For More Information 337

INTRODUCTION

When I first started learning Perl, I actually thought Perl was an evil plot. The syntax tends to the obscure and obtuse and is just plain difficult to master. You'll find lots of bizarre syntax, such as the ubiquitous $_, which does more to prove theories of alien abductions than anything else. Perl is a very flexible language that allows for many ways to get any job done. In the Perl community, this is considered a good thing. The key is finding a successful way to get your job done.

And, that's why I wrote this book. My goal in writing *Cross-Platform Perl* is to free you from experiencing the same problems I did. Let's face it; Perl is hard. So, in the chapters to follow, you'll see an easy, straightforward introduction to Perl. This book goes far beyond the Perl basics, tackling the tough issues that you'll need to solve to get your work done. I'll tell you where Perl really is evil and how you can get around it. I also provide a lot of handy Perl routines you can reuse repeatedly, not only as examples to learn from but in your actual work. And, I'll try to shed some light on the confusion that is Perl. Some of my colleagues tell me that learning Perl is easy—they've done it many times. Perl doesn't have to be difficult if you avoid the confusing constructs. If you've ever been intimidated by Perl, this is the book for you.

This book is intended for a wide-ranging audience that wants to learn Perl, including:

- System administrators
- Anyone requiring a batch or script file that runs on multiple platforms
- Web-page designers who want to add interactive forms or automate Web-page maintenance
- Power users on Windows NT or UNIX who want to automate tasks
- Programmers who develop for UNIX and Windows NT

You don't need any previous programming experience to use Perl effectively. If you have programmed before, you'll find that Perl follows a lot of conventions of the C programming language.

Perl stands for practical extraction and report language. (Others call it the pathologically eclectic rubbish lister.) Originally designed for system administration tasks, Perl has branched out to tens of thousands of users and just about as many uses. Some of the main uses include creating commons gateway interface (CGI) scripts for Web pages, automating system administration tasks, generating reports, and facilitating cross-platform development, such as compilation scripts for UNIX and Windows NT. Perl is free and available for many platforms. Perl is a great tool to automate tasks quickly, especially with its strong text-handling capability.

Created by Larry Wall, Perl grew out of problems with **sed**, **awk**, and other UNIX tools. UNIX system administrators in particular try to get reports on the status of their systems. There's a lot of data to generate these reports, but typically the data are in very obscure formats. So, Perl combines **awk**'s report creation facilities with **sed**'s editing and data manipulation, with lots of other stuff thrown in. What makes Perl especially strong is that you can do a lot more with Perl—and have an easier time at it—than you can with standard UNIX shells or MS-DOS prompts.

Perl is a scripting language, which means you don't have to compile and link Perl programs. Instead, you tell the Perl interpreter to execute your scripts. This makes Perl quite popular for developing quick solutions to smaller administration tasks. Since Perl scripts are stored in text files, you can use any text editor to create your scripts, including **Notepad**, **WordPad**, **Word**, **vi**, or **emacs**. In addition, a Perl package called **Perl/Tk** allows you to create graphical interfaces using the **Tk** toolkit, originally from another scripting language called Tcl. With **Perl/Tk**, you can create a user-friendly front end for your scripts, based on the popular **Tk** toolkit.

Using Perl for Cross-Platform Development

Unlike this book, most Perl books assume that you're running on UNIX and, in some cases, even a particular version of UNIX. I beg to differ. This book is called *Cross-Platform Perl* for a reason. In my work, I must deal with

3

many computer systems with many architectures. Chances are that you face similar challenges. If not, you probably will soon, unless the computer industry stops changing at such a rapid pace. While I'd love to be able to refuse to work on architectures I consider subpar, that isn't a realistic option. Aside from the fact that I consider *all* existing computer architectures subpar, I wouldn't be employed very long following such a strategy. So, I'm constantly looking for computer tools that run on more than one platform and can help me get my job done. Perl is one such tool that can go a long way toward automating many system tasks.

Because Perl runs on many platforms, including Windows NT and UNIX, it has the potential of eliminating—or at least hiding—some of the many platform differences you'll encounter. But, you'll gain no benefits if you create your scripts from a UNIX- or Windows-centric point of view. So, the best way to approach Perl is to concentrate on what works on both systems and only where necessary delve into system-specific details.

Because Perl is a scripting language, this isn't easy. Much of what you'll do from Perl is launch system programs, and these programs differ widely between UNIX and Windows NT, as shown in Chapter 6. Wherever there are platform differences, you'll see one of the following two symbols.

WINDOWS

The Windows icon identifies things specific to Windows NT.

U N I X

The UNIX icon identifies things specific to UNIX.

But, for the vast majority of the book, you'll see no symbols. That's because the vast majority of Perl runs fine on both systems.

In addition to the Windows and UNIX notes, a few more icons can alert you to important points.

C

The C icon identifies tips specially for C and C++ programmers. While you don't require any programming background to use Perl effectively, many Perl scripters come from the realm of programming.

4

The Perl syntax hews *very* close to that of C but diverges in important areas. Don't be fooled by how similar Perl is to C. This icon identifies areas where C programmers will note important syntax differences.

The Note icon indicates something that demands special attention.

The Warning icon warns you about actions that could be hazardous to your Perl scripting career, causing your scripts to run awry and perhaps destroy data.

The CD-ROMs icon refers to items found on the CD-ROMs that accompany this book.

When to Use Perl

There's an abundance of scripting and programming languages. Everything from Java to Visual Basic to Tcl to C++ to Ada and even Object COBOL competes for our attention and use. With so many languages, you have to decide how many you have time to learn and when to use a particular tool.

My philosophy is simple: use the tool that works best for you. FORTRAN 77 may truly work better for your task at hand. When examining Perl, some factors you should consider include:

- Perl has extensive text-handling, searching, sorting, and manipulation capabilities. It works well for dealing with data in text files.
- Perl provides very useful report-generation constructs.
- Perl interfaces to most system services, especially on UNIX. Perl includes commands for DBM file access, networking, and accessing UNIX password files.
- Perl scripts run on Windows and UNIX, allowing you to write one script for multiple platforms.

- Many modules available for Perl provide extensive support for Web-page access and connectivity to major applications such as Oracle and Informix databases.

The main drawback to Perl is its cryptic syntax. Perl allows you to take many shortcuts, saving you time but creating nearly unreadable scripts. With Perl, you don't have to create unreadable scripts, so I recommend staying away from most of the Perl shortcuts.

As always, use the tool that works best for you. If you'd prefer to write everything in C++ or Java, use that. If you'd prefer Bourne shell scripts, use that.

Perl Versions

As of this writing, the current version of Perl is Perl 5. On UNIX, it's at version 5.002, but on Windows it remains at 5.001. There's a great deal of differences between Perl 4, the last major release, and Perl 5. This book covers Perl 5 (which is included on the accompanying CD-ROMs), but most of the material should work with Perl 4 as well.

Perl 5 has surprising differences between the minor versions, such as Perl 5.000, Perl 5.001, and Perl 5.002. You may have Perl 5, but the differences between the seemingly minor release may actually be major. Because of this, all the examples were tested under Perl 5.002 and Perl 5.001. All the material here will work on Perl 5.001, unless otherwise noted.

Acquiring Perl

You can acquire Perl on the accompanying CD-ROMs or over the Internet. But, before you spend time acquiring and installing Perl, it's a good idea to see if you already have Perl installed. To check this, try the following command at either the UNIX shell or the Windows MS-DOS prompt:

```
perl -v
```

6

If Perl is installed, you should get a message back from the Perl interpreter that tells you which version of Perl you have installed. To most effectively use this book, you want Perl version 5 or later.

If you get an error message, chances are you don't have Perl installed. In that case, you'll want to install Perl from the CD-ROM that accompany this book.

Installing Perl from the CD-ROMs

The CD-ROM that comes with this book contain the latest (as of this writing) version of Perl, as well as a number of handy Perl scripts and packages, including **Perl/Tk**.

The means to install Perl differ between UNIX and Windows.

WINDOWS

Installing Perl on Windows NT and Windows 95: On Windows NT or Windows 95, Perl comes precompiled in binary format. Copy all the files from the **win** directory on the CD-ROMs, or use PKZip for Windows, WinZip, or another ZIP archive program to extract the files from the ZIP archive for Windows, whichever method you prefer. However, you must use a modern ZIP program that can handle the long file names and directories in the Perl **ZIP** file.

These files should be copied to your hard disk in a directory named **\perl**. You can place Perl in other locations, but it really wants to go in **\perl**.

Once placed on your hard disk, follow the instructions in the **INSTALL.TXT** file and then run the **INSTALL.BAT** batch file.

Perl is a command-line engine, so you'll need to run Perl from the MS-DOS command prompt.

U N I X

Installing Perl on UNIX: To install Perl on UNIX, you'll need to compile the source code of Perl, which is written in the C language. To do this, you must have a C compiler on your system. A C compiler has been standard equipment on UNIX systems; however, many UNIX vendors now skimp in this regard.

If that's the case, you can get a freeware C compiler, the GNU C compiler, from **ftp://prep.ai.mit.edu** on the Internet.

Once you ensure that you have a C compiler, look on the CD-ROM in the **perl** directory, which contains the Perl sources. Copy the files to your hard disk into a directory (you can choose which directory). You're now ready to configure Perl for your system.

Because Perl allows you to perform many system-level tasks, it needs to know a lot about your system. Luckily, a script called **Configure** can figure out most of the system dependencies on its own.

Change to the directory you copied the Perl source code to, which is the top-level Perl directory. The task of the configuration is to build a file named **config.sh**. So, if you see a file named **config.sh**, remove it or copy it to a different name.

Next, run the **Configure** script. This is a Bourne shell script that you run with the normal **sh** command:

```
sh Configure
```

This script will ask you a lot of questions, starting with your platform. Normally, it guesses well, such as guessing a platform of *linux* on a Linux system.

You'll also need to specify the installation directory. For this, the default is **/usr/bin**. I normally don't like placing commands like **perl** in system directories, but this has been the Perl convention for quite some time. You can use a different installation directory, but you'll find that, on installing Perl, the **make** scripts want to install Perl in **/usr/bin/perl**, the default location where many Perl scripts expect to find the **perl** command. (The **make** command is used as a master control system to choose which Perl source files to compile and how to link the final application.)

For the rest of the questions from **Configure**, you can accept the defaults. If you don't know the answer, either try to find out the answer or just accept the defaults. If anything goes wrong, you can always try to configure Perl again. Generally, the process goes pretty quickly if you accept the answers the **Configure** script determines on its own.

After configuring Perl for your system, you need to run **make** to compile all the source code (in C) and then create Perl on your system. Use the **make** command:

```
make
```

When Perl is built, you should test it out to see if things are fine. To test Perl, run the following command:

```
make test
```

If any problems arise, you'll need to look into them. You may need to run **sh Configure** again to change some options.

If everything works well, the next step is to install Perl:

```
make install
```

This command installs Perl where you specified in the configuration. You'll need to have write permissions on the directories you install Perl to, for example, **/usr/local/bin** or **/usr/bin**.

Updating to Newer Versions: In the fast-paced world of computer technology, there's always a danger whenever you make a CD-ROM like the one that accompanies this book. No matter what, sooner or later a new version will appear. When that happens, don't worry, you can always pick up any later version of Perl from **http://www.perl.com/perl/info/software.html**, part of the Perl Home Page on the World Wide Web. In addition, my Perl Web page maintains a set of the latest versions of Perl and the Perl packages covered in this book, such as **perl/Tk**. See the Perl page at **http://ourworld.compuserve.com/homepages/efjohnson/perl.htm** for the links.

With this, you should be ready to learn Perl starting in Chapter 1.

Learning Perl

Cross-Platform Perl contains two major sections: Learning Perl and Advanced Perl. The first section of the book concentrates on learning Perl, covering the basics of the Perl language and how to use Perl to perform common tasks like working with files, creating reports, and launching applications.

The second section builds on the first and covers Perl usage for a number of advanced tasks, such as creating CGI scripts for Web pages, facilitating cross-platform software development, working with client-server applications, and creating graphical interfaces.

There's a lot more to Perl than any one book can cover. The language keeps growing, and new modules appear every day. What I've tried to do is focus on the most important and useful constructs in Perl, especially constructs that work on a number of platforms. Once you master the material in this book, the extensive online Perl reference material should take you the rest of the way. In addition, Appendix A contains an extensive list of books and online material that I found the most useful for working with Perl.

Contacting the Author

The best way to contact me is through my Web page on the Internet, at **http://www.pconline.com/~erc**, where you'll also find more information on Perl and links to the latest versions of useful Perl modules.

Learning Perl

This section introduces the Perl language and how you can create scripts in Perl.

The first chapter briefly introduces Perl and provides a few short Perl scripts. Then, starting in Chapter 2, you'll get a full dose of the basics of the Perl language.

Since the vast majority of computer tasks revolve around files, working with files gets its own chapter. Chapter 3 also covers differences in file naming between Windows NT and UNIX, which is made even more difficult because of the Perl convention that uses the backslash character, \, as a special character.

One of the strongest, yet weirdest, areas of Perl lies in regular expressions, which are covered in Chapter 4. You'll use regular expressions to break out information from lines of text and substitute new next. For example, regular expressions are very useful for breaking apart and reformatting data to create reports or query a database and then displaying the results in a Web page.

Once you've mastered regular expressions, the next task is to use the data you've broken down into component parts and then combine the data in a new way to generate reports. You can use reports for summarizing system resource usage, extracting data from other sources (such as databases), and simply formatting information you have to make the information more useful. Chapter 5 shows how to do all this and more.

A common task in any scripting language is launching other applications. You may want a Perl script that starts a backup or initiates the C compiler. Chapter 6 covers Perl's ability to launch applications and control processes and highlights the differences between UNIX and Windows NT versions of Perl in this regard.

Chapter 7 rounds out the discussion of Perl basics, delving into the Perl concept of a package. A package combines a set of Perl routines, some written in C and some in Perl, into one unit that you can load into your Perl scripts. Packages are used for database access and system administration and in writing CGI Web scripts.

CHAPTER 1

Beginning with Perl

This chapter covers:

- Starting to program in Perl
- A first Perl script
- Running Perl scripts
- Getting input from the user
- If statements to control flow
- Making an executable command from Perl scripts
- Launching Perl scripts from the Windows **Explorer** or **Program Manager**

Perl, the practical extraction and report language, is an extremely powerful and complicated language, as reflected in Perl's official slogan: *There's More Than One Way to Do It.* That means there's a lot of material to cover when learning Perl. Luckily, you don't have to do much in Perl before you write commands. Other programming languages, like C and Java, require that you provide a lot more information about your program. You need to declare variables to be of certain types and set up functions to be called a particular way, but not so with Perl. You don't need to pre-declare variables in Perl. You just start writing commands. Perl differentiates most variables by the data you place in the variable, such as text or numerics.

In this chapter, we'll create a few Perl programs, introducing the syntax so that you can gradually get a handle on what Perl is all about.

A First Perl Script

The simplest Perl script is the ubiquitous Hello World script, which follows:

```
#
# hello.pl
#
# Hello World in Perl.
print "Hello World.\n";
```

Enter this program using any text editor and then save the file as **hello.pl**. All Perl programs are simply text files that get passed to the Perl command. I use *.pl* as an extension for all Perl scripts. While you can certainly use any extension, **.pl** remains the most common extension in the Perl community.

WINDOWS

If you're using the scripts from the CD-ROM, you'll want to use the **Write** or **Wordpad** editors, rather than **Notepad**. **Notepad** doesn't handle the UNIX style of newline characters very well, while both **Write** and **Wordpad** can deal with different characters that end the line.

The basic issue is that UNIX uses a newline character to end each line, while Windows wants both a carriage return and a newline. With **Write** or **Wordpad**, you won't notice the difference.

Running Perl Programs

To run this program from a shell or MS-DOS prompt, use the following command:

```
perl hello.pl
```

When you run this command, you should see the following highly original output:

```
Hello World.
```

If you get an error message stating that the Perl command is not found, then either you haven't installed Perl or the Perl command is not in your command path. You command path lists the directories where your system looks for commands. On both UNIX and Windows, you need to extend the *PATH* environment variable. See the Introduction for more on installing Perl.

Perl is a text-based language. Whenever you run a Perl script, you need to be in an MS-DOS prompt window, as shown in Figure 1.1. Most of what Perl does is inherently text-based, which, of course, flies in the face of the graphical Windows environment. See Chapter 12 for more on creating graphical interfaces with **Perl/Tk**.

Figure 1.1 Running Perl in an MS-DOS prompt window.

The First Program in Depth

To give you a better understanding of Perl, I'll go through each of the statements in the **hello.pl** Perl script.

Any line starting with a # indicates a comment. Such comments have no effect on program execution. Because Perl scripts are compiled to a byte-code format and then executed, parsing comments does not effect program execution as much as it would with Bourne shell scripts or MS-DOS batch files.

You can also place a # in the middle of a line, as shown here:

```
print "Wow.\n";    # This is a comment in a line.
```

Everything from the # to the end of the line is a comment.

While comments may seem to be only for your edification, I can't stress enough the need to comment. Comments not only tell you what you intend the Perl script to do, but they also tell others who use the scripts what the scripts are intended for. If you write a script now and come back to it in a few months, you'll be grateful if you commented the tricky parts of the script.

Furthermore, if problems appear in your scripts, comments can help you figure out what the problem area was supposed to do and track down the problems.

That's enough preaching. Perl statements end with a semicolon, ;. Each command you add will need a semicolon at the end.

You don't necessarily have to stick to one command per line. Some commands extend over more than one line, and you may sometimes want to place more than one command on a line. Perl is very open in this regard. Just remember that a semicolon ends each command.

The Print Command

While seemingly very simple, the `print` command is one of the most important commands in Perl. If you think about it for a moment, you'll realize that, with the `print` command, you can:

- Tell the user what your Perl script is doing. This is very important for long-running scripts. Users are often impatient and fearful that the script or the system isn't working properly.

- Ask the user for information.

- Help track down problems by printing extra information for your eyes only.

- Generate output to be stored in a file or used for other purposes, such as common gateway interface (CGI) scripts that create information for Web pages.

The `print` command prints out the text you provide it. C programmers will recognize the special sequence, \n, which indicates a newline.

The backslash comes from the C language and is a form of *escape*. The backslash gets us around the problem of distinguishing between characters that mean things to Perl and characters we want to print out, such as an end-of-line marker (a newline) or a tab. Table 1.1 lists other backslash escapes used in Perl.

Table 1.1 Backslash escapes in Perl.

Perl	Usage
\\	Allow the use of a backslash.
\"	Double quote.
\a	Bell.
\b	Backspace.
\c*N*	Any control character (e.g., \cC for **Control-C**).
\e	Escape character (character 27).
\E	End a sequence of \L or \U.
\f	Formfeed.
\l	Make the next character lowercase.
\L	Make following characters lowercase until \E.
\n	Newline.
\r	Return.
\t	Tab.
\u	Make the next character uppercase.
\U	Make following characters uppercase until \E.
\0*NN*	Any octal numeric value.
\x*NN*	Any hexadecimal numeric value.

UNIX uses a forward slash, /, to separate directory names, while Windows uses a backward slash, \ to do the same job. But, as you can see, the backslash has a special meaning in Perl (and many other programming languages for that matter). Consequently, you'll often have to use the two-backslash construct, \\, to enter the real backslash that you want.

Our first Perl script, **hello.pl**, merely displays output for the user. Extending this, our next Perl script will delve further into user interaction and ask the user a question.

Getting Input in Perl Scripts

A good number of the Perl scripts you write will need to get input—somehow—from the user. One of the simplest ways to do this is to print out a question, using the `print` command, and then read the answer from the keyboard. (Chapter 12 delves into more advanced graphical user interfaces using **Perl/Tk**.)

The next script, **asklang.pl**, asks what the user's favorite scripting language is (and we all know the answer to that, right?). Enter the following script and save it as **asklang.pl**:

```
#
# asklang.pl
#
# Perl script that asks a question and
# gets user response.
#
# Note the extra space to print out.
print "What is your favorite scripting language? ";

$lang = <STDIN>;

chomp($lang);

if ( $lang eq "Perl" ) {
    print "Congratulations, you chose Perl!\n";
```

```
} else {
    print "Well, use $lang if you feel ";
    print "it's the right tool for the job\n";
}
```

When you run this script, you'll be asked the following question:

```
What is your favorite scripting language?
```

Depending on your answer, you'll get different results, such as the following:

```
C:\perl> perl asklang.pl
What is your favorite scripting language? Perl
Congratulations, you choose Perl!
```

```
C:\perl> perl asklang.pl
What is your favorite scripting language? APL
Well, use APL if you feel it's the right tool for the job
```

If you don't answer the question properly, it prints out a sarcastic response (a true advancement in user interface design, of course).

Starting with the first `print` command, you'll notice that this `print` statement has no `\n` to indicate an end of line. This ensures that the user's response appears on the same line as the question.

The next line, `$lang = <STDIN>;`, introduces Perl's variables.

Perl Variables

Perl, like virtually all computer languages, allows you to store data in variables. In the **asklang.pl** script, `$lang` indicates that *lang* is a variable. The leading dollar sign, `$`, indicates that this variable is a scalar variable and holds a single value.

Scalars in Perl include a single number or character string. Another class of Perl variables, *array* variables, allow a group of numbers or text strings. For example, a line of text in a file is normally considered a scalar value, while all the lines of text in a file are considered an array.

To set a variable, use the = operator, as follows:

```
# Setting scalar variables.
$var = "Text";
$number_var = 44.5;
# var1.pl
```

You'll see a lot more about Perl's variables in Chapter 2.

Standard Input

The **asklang.pl** script, gets user input from STDIN. This concept comes from UNIX, where all programs have three open files: STDIN (input), STDOUT (output), and STDERR (error output). At a UNIX terminal (or terminal window), STDIN normally comes from your keyboard. Data entered at the keyboard get sent to the application as if they came from the file ID of STDIN. (UNIX treats almost everything as a file.) Similarly, the STDOUT and STDERR file IDs are tied to the terminal's display. Data output via STDOUT or STDERR is sent to the terminal.

NOTE Error messages get sent to STDERR, while normal output goes to STDOUT. This allows you to redirect the output of a command to a file while still seeing error messages on your screen.

With Perl, your programs can open files (you'll do this quite a lot) using the open command (see Chapter 3), or you can use one of the predefined file handles, including STDIN, STDOUT, and STDERR. A *file handle* is the means by which your Perl scripts access files. The angle brackets, < and >, read data from the file handle that is placed between the angle brackets, such as <STDIN>. For example, the following command reads a single line of text from a file, in this case STDIN (the keyboard), and places that line of text into the scalar variable lang:

```
$lang = <STDIN>;
```

In scalar context, as shown previously, the command reads a single line of text from a file. In array context, which is described in Chapter 2, the <STDIN> command would read in an entire file. You always need to be aware of which context your scripts are in. See Chapter 2 for more on this.

UNIX makes a lot of use of text files to store data. Usually each line in a text file is a separate record, sort of like ASCII-delimited dBase databases. Thus, Perl has many commands for working with lines of text.

Chomping the Data

When you read in a line of text with the $lang = <STDIN> statement, Perl places the entire line of text, including the trailing carriage return or newline character, into the variable lang. In most cases, however, this is the wrong thing to do. You don't want extra carriage returns in your data. Furthermore, Windows and UNIX use different means to signify an end of line, so this introduces portability problems. Consequently, you'll normally use the chomp command to chomp off this extra data:

```
chomp($lang);
```

The chomp command is configured on each system to use the system's default characters for indicating an end of line. On UNIX, this is the newline character. On Windows, this is a carriage return character and then a newline character.

On older versions of Perl scripts, especially UNIX-specific versions of Perl, you'll often see the chop command remove the UNIX newline character at the end of data input. The chop command is like the chomp command, except that chop—the older command—simply removes the last character of the string. If you allow your scripts to run only on UNIX, then the last character is indeed the end-of-line marker (a newline character). You'll find that this won't work on Windows, which uses two characters to end each line. So, I stick to using chomp in place of chop.

Using If to Control the Flow of Your Scripts

Like virtually all programming or scripting languages, Perl provides an if statement. The if statement checks whether a condition is true. If so, it executes the next statement or block.

From the **asklang.pl** script, the following is an example of an if statement:

```
if ( $lang eq "perl" ) {
    print "Congratulations, you chose perl!\n";
}
```

The curly braces indicate a *block* in Perl, a means of grouping a number of statements together.

Unlike C, you must use the curly braces in a block.

You can extend the if statement to include an else block. This gets executed if the condition *isn't* true.

In the **asklang.pl** script, the else condition prints out a neutral message (I don't want to get into language wars) if you decide Perl isn't your favorite scripting language, as shown here:

```
if ( $lang eq "Perl" ) {
    print "Congratulations, you chose Perl!\n";
} else {
    print "Well, use $lang if you feel ";
    print "it's the right tool for the job\n";
}
```

You can also use an elsif to check whether a different condition is true, as shown here:

```
if ( $lang eq "Perl" ) {
    print "Congratulations, you chose Perl!\n";
} elsif ( $lang eq "Tcl" ) {
        print "Tcl is great, too.\n";
```

```
} else {
    print "Well, use $lang if you feel ";
    print "it's the right tool for the job\n";
}
```

WARNING

That's elsif, *not* elseif. This is yet another quirk of the Perl language.

In summary, the if syntax follows:

```
if (condition) {
    # ...
}
```

```
if (condition) {
    # ...
} else {
    # ...
}
```

```
if (condition) {
    # ...
} elsif (condition) {
} else {
    # ...
}
```

If Expressions

The if statement evaluates an expression. If that expression is true, then the if parts get executed. If not, then the else part or any elsif parts get evaluated. The expression in this case is ($lang eq "Perl"). As you'd expect, this checks whether the value held in the *lang* variable equals the string "Perl". The eq operator performs a string equality check and returns 1 (true) if the two strings are equal or 0 (false) if they are not.

Perl has a number of string comparison operators that you can use in if statements, as shown in Table 1.2. These operators appear to have come from the FORTRAN language.

Table 1.2 String comparisons.

Perl	Usage
eq	Equal.
ge	Greater than or equal to.
gt	Greater than.
le	Less than or equal to.
lt	Less than.
ne	Not equal.
cmp	Returns -1 if less than, 0 if equal, and 1 if greater than.

All string comparisons are done by the numeric values of the characters. For example, an uppercase A has an ASCII value of 65, which makes it less than an uppercase B, which has an ASCII value of 66.

In addition to string comparisons, Perl allows for numeric comparisons, using the operators shown in Table 1.3.

Table 1.3 Numeric comparison.

Perl	Usage
==	Equal.
!=	Not equal.
<	Less than.
<=	Less than or equal to.
>	Greater than.
>=	Greater than or equal to.
<=>	Returns -1 if less than, 0 if equal, and 1 if greater than.

C programmers should recognize most of these numeric operators right away.

How Perl Runs Programs

When Perl first tries to run a script, it parses the entire script, compiling your commands into an internal format, and then executes the script from this internal format. As a result, most errors in the script, especially syntax errors, get reported before the script starts to run. This is very different from other scripting languages like most UNIX shells or the MS-DOS prompt, which parse each line separately and report errors only when actually executing a command. This usually helps you detect errors in your script in advance, but sometimes errors remain undetected in this parsing stage.

Problems with Perl Scripts

To show how Perl detects problems, we can simply make an intentional error in a Perl script. We all probably have more than enough problems with unintentional errors to consider adding errors on purpose, but this example should help you track down the inevitable problems in Perl scripts.

One of the most common problems is forgetting a semicolon at the end of a Perl command. To show this, let's take the **asklang.pl** script used previously and remove the semicolon after the chomp command, as shown in the following **problem1.pl** script:

```
#
# problem1.pl
#
# perl script that asks a question and
# gets user response.
#
# THIS SCRIPT HAS AN ERROR.
# YOUR MISSION IS TO FIND THIS ERROR.
#
# Note the extra space to print out.
```

```
print "What is your favorite scripting language? ";

$lang = <STDIN>;

# NOTE MISSING SEMICOLON BELOW.
chomp($lang)

if ( $lang eq "Perl" ) {
    print "Congratulations, you chose Perl!\n";
} else {
        print "Well, use $lang if you feel ";
        print "it's the right tool for the job\n";
}
```

26

When you run this script, you'll see the following error:

```
syntax error at problem1.pl line 20, near "}"
Execution of problem1.pl aborted due to compilation errors.
```

WARNING

A very common problem when learning Perl is forgetting the semicolon at the end of each command. If you do this, chances are that Perl will report an error. The tough part is that Perl detects the error only *after* the line where the problem really occurred. So, when Perl reports a syntax error, the line number given is often only a guide. The error may well have occurred on a line prior to the one listed.

In the **problem1.pl** script, the error is really that the chomp command doesn't end with a semicolon. Yet, the error reported appears to be at the end of the if-else statement.

Finding Out More about Perl's Commands

One of the best ways to track down problems in your Perl scripts is to look at the online documentation. Perl comes with extensive online documentation. In UNIX terms, this information is stored as online manual pages, which are accessible from the UNIX **man** or **xman** commands and shown in Figure 1.2.

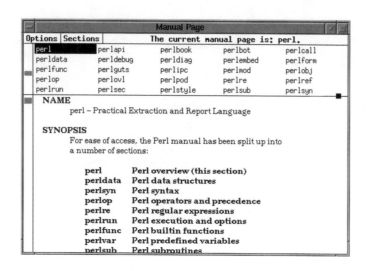

Figure 1.2 Looking up Perl documentation with **xman**.

On Windows NT, you need to use a Web browser, such as **Internet Explorer** or **Navigator**, since the Perl documents appear as HTML (Hyper Text Markup Language) files in the Win32 version of Perl. Figure 1.3 shows an example.

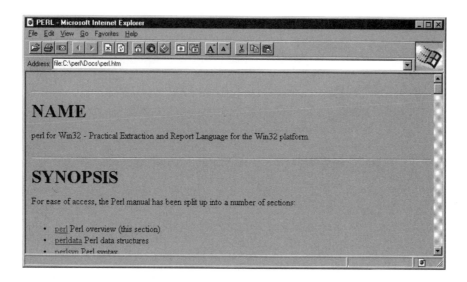

Figure 1.3 Browsing the Perl Web pages on Windows.

These Web pages are available on the CD-ROM for use on both UNIX and Windows (or any other platform you desire) in the doc directory.

CD-ROM

28

Table 1.4 lists the available topics of information.

Table 1.4 Online reference information on Perl.

man Topic	Covers
oleauto	Perl OLE automation on Windows (see Chapter 7)
perl	Main Perl overview
perlapi	Perl C application programming interface and glue routines
perlbook	List of some Perl books (see Appendix A)
perlbot	Object-oriented tricks and examples
perlcall	Calling conventions from C
perldata	Data structures
perldebug	Debugging
perldiag	Diagnostic messages
perlembed	How to embed Perl in your C or C++ application
perlform	Formats (see Chapter 5)
perlfunc	Built-in functions
perlguts	Internal functions for those doing extensions
perlipc	Interprocess communication
perlmod	Modules
perlobj	Objects
perlop	Operators and precedence
perlovl	Overloading semantics
perlpod	Plain old documentation
perlre	Regular expressions
perlref	References and nested data structures

`perlrun`	Execution and options
`perlsub`	Subroutines
`perlsec`	Security
`perlstyle`	Style guide
`perlsyn`	Syntax
`perltrap`	Traps for the unwary
`perlvar`	Predefined variables
`win32`	Overview of Win32 issues for Perl
`win32ext`	Miscellaneous Win32 extensions to Perl

Making Your Scripts into Commands

On both Windows and UNIX, you can convert your Perl scripts into commands that can be executed from the UNIX command line or the Windows **Explorer**. Unfortunately, the methods differ on UNIX and Windows.

Making an Executable Script: On UNIX, virtually all scripting languages (including Perl), use the # character to mark the start of a comment. (Some scripting languages require that the # be in the first column.) In most UNIX shell scripts, you'll usually see a strange comment on the very first line:

```
#!/bin/sh
```

This comment tells the command shell you're running in, usually **csh** or **ksh**, which program to run to execute the script (in this case, **/bin/sh**). This is a handy way to request that a shell script be run under the interpreter for which it was designed. For example, I use the C shell (**csh**) for my daily work, but virtually all UNIX shell scripts are written in the Bourne shell (**sh**) language. This initial comment tells my **csh** to run **sh** for the script (rather than running another copy of **csh**).

This is just a convention, but it is followed on most UNIX command shells like **sh, csh**, and **ksh**. Because this convention is so widely followed, you can take advantage of this to ask the shell (usually **csh** or **ksh**) to run Perl. This allows you to type in the name of a Perl script alone, like `hello.pl`, and have it execute, instead of typing `perl hello.pl`.

To do this, form a comment that notes the location of your Perl command usually the following:

```
#!/usr/bin/perl
```

You need to add this line to your Perl scripts, as the very first line in the file.

If you installed Perl in a different location, you'll need to change this comment. Once you place the starting comment (and it must be the first line in the script), the next step is to make your Perl script as an executable file. In UNIX, an executable file has a file name that you can type in as a command. To do this, use the **chmod** command:

```
chmod +x hello.pl
```

You should now be able to execute your script from the UNIX command line:

```
hello.pl
```

If you have any problems, your command shell may not support this convention. If so, you'll probably get a number of errors, because Perl commands are not compatible with most UNIX shell commands (some are, which can lead to interesting results if you execute a Perl script as a Bourne shell script).

There's one main problem with this special first-line comment: some systems, especially Hewlett-Packard's HP-UX, allow only 32 characters in the path. Thus, long paths like **/usr5/local /perl/src/perl5.002/bin** won't work.

WINDOWS

Double-Clicking to Launch Your Perl Scripts: On Windows, you can use the **Explorer** to associate Perl with your scripts. The easiest way to do this is to follow a consistent naming convention for your Perl scripts. Windows likes best if you use a consistent suffix, such as *.pl*, on all your Perl scripts.

In the **Explorer**, select a Perl script file, such as **hello.pl**. Then, from the File menu, choose **Open With**. If Perl appears in the list of applications, select it. Otherwise, the **Other** button will let you browse your hard disk and find the Perl executable (**perl.exe**). When you find Perl, then select it and be sure the flag is set to always use Perl to open the file.

Figure 1.4 shows the window where you select Perl.

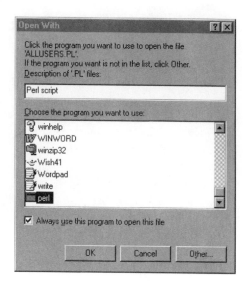

Figure 1.4 Associating Perl with Perl scripts.

In the older **Program Manager**, you can create a program icon to launch Perl and your script.

Summary

Perl scripts are text files with Perl commands, the simplest of which is the print command, which allows you to print out data for the user.

The print command outputs data to the user. You can get the user's response by reading input from <STDIN> into a variable.

Perl denotes variables by a leading $, such as $var. The if statement allows you to control the flow of your Perl scripts. You'll see a number of other statements, such as while and for, in Chapter 2.

With this chapter, you've now become a multifaceted Perl affectiondo. In Chapter 2, we'll cover a lot more about variables, scalar and array data, as well as flesh out the basics of Perl.

Perl Commands Introduced in This Chapter

```
chomp
chop
if
print
```

Perl Basics

This chapter covers:

- Controlling your scripts
- Math operations
- Operations on text
- Variables and arrays
- Scalar variables
- Associative arrays
- Built-in variables
- Accessing command-line arguments
- Subroutines

The Perl You Need to Know

Perl's syntax seems arbitrarily complex, abbreviated, and obscure. Even so, learning a few simple basics will get you up to speed and allow you to take advantage of the majority of Perl's capabilities.

In this chapter, we'll tackle the basics of the Perl language, expanding on the introduction to Perl in Chapter 1.

Controlling Your Perl Scripts

In addition to the if statement introduced in Chapter 1, Perl offers a host of other commands to control the flow of your Perl scripts.

The while command loops while a condition is true:

```
while (condition) {
  # ...
}
```

For example:

```
# Example of the while statement.
$i = 0;
while ($i < 10) {
    print "Iteration $i.\n";
    $i++;
}
# while1.pl
```

Always ensure that your while loops eventually terminate. It's up to you to figure out a way. Most often, this is done by incrementing or decrementing a variable each iteration of the loop, as shown previously.

WARNING

You can reverse the test with the until statement:

```
until (condition) {
  # ...
}
```

With until, you need to ensure that the test is set up properly, as shown here:

```
# Example of the until statement.
$i = 0;
```

```
#
# Note reversed test.
#
until ($i >= 10) {
    print "Iteration $i.\n";
    $i++;
}
# until1.pl
```

This use of `until` diverges from C and even Pascal practice.

The `unless` statement is the opposite of `if` and executes a block unless a condition is true.

```
unless (condition) {
    # ...
}
```

or:

```
unless (condition) {
    # ...
} else {
    # ...
}
```

You can use a `for` loop, to loop for a number of times, as shown next:

```
for (initialization; expression; continue) {
    # ...
}
```

The *initialization* part gets executed first and normally initializes the loop variable to zero or 1. The *expression* is checked on each iteration through the loop. If true, `for` iterates again. The *continue* gets executed at the end of the loop, just before the *expression* is evaluated again. The *continue* part usually increments the loop-controlling variable.

This `for` loop comes straight from C. To have a loop iterate 10 times, you can follow the C language convention:

```
# Example of the for statement.
for ($i = 0; $i < 10; $i++) {
    print "Iteration $i.\n";
}
# for1.pl
```

Note that unlike the `while` and `until` statements, with `for` you don't need to increment the loop-controlling variable, in this case *i*. The `for` statement has a section for this at the top of the loop.

Similar to `for`, the `foreach` statement lets you iterate for each element in a list or array:

```
foreach variable (list) {
  # ...
}
```

Each time through the loop, `foreach` places the an element of the list into the scalar variable, repeating until all the elements in the list have been processed. For example:

```
# Example of foreach.
@languages = ("Perl","Tcl","Java","Oberon","python");

foreach $lang (@languages) {

    if ($lang eq "Perl") {
        print "The most wonderful language is $lang.\n";
    } else {
        print "$lang has some neat ideas.\n";
    }
}
# foreach.pl
```

When you run this script, you'll see the following output:

```
The most wonderful language is Perl.
Tcl has some neat ideas.
Java has some neat ideas.
Oberon has some neat ideas.
python has some neat ideas.
```

You can also use the .. operator, which goes from a minimum to a maximum, with foreach, as shown here:

```
# Example of foreach from a min to a max.
foreach $i (5..10) {
    print "$i\n";
}
# foreach2.pl
```

See the section on arrays later in this chapter for more examples using foreach.

Continuing

Perl also allows for a strange continue block. In a loop, the continue block gets executed just before the condition gets evaluated again, as shown next:

```
while (condition) {
  # ...
} continue {
  # ..
}
```

For example, the following while loop is equivalent to the **while1.pl** example:

```
# Example of while with continue.
$i = 0;
while ($i < 10) {
```

```
    print "Iteration $i.\n";

} continue {

    $i++;

}
# while2.pl
```

Normally, you increment a variable in the `continue` block. You can also increment the variable inside the main block, as shown previously in the **while1.pl** example. The reason for a `continue` block is Perl's extra flow control statements.

Extra Flow Control

Table 2.1 lists some extra flow control commands.

Table 2.1 Extra Perl flow control commands.

Command	Usage
goto *label*	Jumps to named *label*.
last	Breaks out of the current innermost loop.
last *label*	Breaks out of current loop at *label*.
next	Starts next iteration of loop.
next *label*	Starts next iteration of loop, at *label*.
redo	Restarts the loop without re-evaluating condition.
redo *label*	Restarts the loop *label* without re-evaluating condition.

NOTE `Goto` **Considered Harmful**: Way back in 1966, a computer scientist named Edsger Dijkstra became famous for a letter attacking the use of `goto` commands. Since `goto` allows the control flow to jump to anywhere, this makes programs of any sort, including Perl scripts, harder to debug and maintain. Luckily, Perl gives you the ability to revisit this ancient controversy and prove it wrong.

You can insert labels at the start of most loops and flow control statements, as shown in Table 2.2.

Table 2.2 Perl flow control in brief.

Command

```
if (condition) { } elsif (condition) { } else { }
unless (condition) { } else { }
label: while (condition) { } continue { }
label: until (condition) { } continue { }
label: for (intialization; expression; continue) { }
label: foreach variable (list) { }
label: { } continue { }
do { } while condition;
do { } until condition;
do { }
```

Most parts of the commands in Table 2.2, such as the `continue` block, are optional.

Surprisingly enough, Perl has no `switch` statement; Perl has everything else imaginable. The reason for this is that you are free to implement switch any number of ways, as shown in the Perl online documentation. (This is called a teaser to get you to look at the extensive Perl information available online.)

Ending Modifiers

In another strange twist, you can execute a simple Perl statement if a condition is true, by reversing the `if` statement syntax:

```
statement; if condition;
```

You can also do this for `unless`, `while`, and `until`:

40

```
statement; unless condition;
statement; while condition;
statement; until condition;
```

With this construct, Perl won't execute the statement unless the condition is met, following the rules already shown for each of `if`, `unless`, `while`, and `until`.

You can also use logical operators in statements, although this leads to odd-looking Perl commands, like the one shown here:

```
# Test of open and die.
$filename = "nofile";

open(TMP, $filename)
    or die "Can't open \"$filename\"";
# opendie.pl
```

The `or` part allows for a statement to get executed if the main part fails, in this case if the `open` command fails to open the file. The `or` part often uses Perl's other `or` syntax, `||`. The `die` command exits the Perl script and prints out an error message to `STDERR`.

Perl doesn't require a newline, `\n`, to end the message passed to the `die` command, because `die` will append extra information to your message, along with a newline. If you place a newline in this message, `die` won't print the extra information.

See Chapter 3 for more on opening files.

Flow control forms one of the basics of Perl. You also need to know about math and text operations.

Math

Perl, like most computer languages, provides a number of math operators, of which the main ones are listed in Table 2.3.

Table 2.3 Math operators.

Operator	Result
$var + value	Add $var and value.
$var - value	Subtract value from $var.
$var * value	Multiply $var times value.
$var / value	Divide $var by value.
$var % value	Divide $var by value, only use remainder.
$var ** value	Return $var to the power of value.

Perl also provides a number of assignment operators, which will be very familiar to C programmers. Table 2.4 lists these assignment operators.

Table 2.4 Assignment operators.

Operator	Result
$var = value	$var gets set to value.
$var += value	$var gets increased by value.
$var -= value	$var gets decreased by value.
$var++	$var gets increased by one, after evaluation.
++$var	$var gets increased by one, before evaluation.
$var--	$var gets decreased by one, after evaluation.
--$var	$var gets decreased by one, before evaluation.

Even though Perl is an interpreted language, its math operations tend to be quite efficient because Perl scripts are compiled to internal byte-codes before execution. This means that math operations tend to execute a lot faster than for strictly interpreted languages, where each statement is parsed one at a time during execution.

Even so, if you intend to perform a lot of computations, Perl is probably not the right tool for the job. Another computer language, such as C++ or FORTRAN, would be more appropriate.

Floating Point: All Perl math operations are performed on double-precision floating-point values (normally 64 bits in size). Perl still makes the value floating point, instead of using an integer, even if you use a simple statement like the following,:

```
$i = 1;
```

For these kinds of simple values, integer math is much more efficient. If you want to use integer math, you can place the following statement in a block (a block goes from opening curly brace, {, to the closing brace, }):
```
use integer;
```

For example:

```
#
# Example of use integer.
#

do {

# Use integer math inside block only.

use integer;
    for ($i = 0; $i < 10; $i++) {
        print "$i\n";
    }
}

# useint.pl
```

You can nest these commands within inner blocks, as in the preceding do block. This enforces integer math until the end of the block. If you want to disable integer math within a block, you can use the following:

```
no integer;
```

The no integer command turns off integer math until the end of the block.

Hexadecimal and Octal Numbers: Like the C language, Perl allows you to format numbers in hexadecimal or octal. An integer with a leading *0* is an octal number. An integer with a leading *0x* (or *0X*) is a hexadecimal number. Like C, Perl uses the letters *A* through *F* to indicate the numbers (in decimal) 10 to 15. For example:

```
# Hex and octal numbers
$hex = 0xFF;
$octal = 010;

print "0xFF = $hex, 010 = $octal.\n";

# hex.pl
```

Math Functions

Perl provides a number of math functions, such as abs for absolute value and cos for cosine. See the **perlfunc** online documentation for an extensive list of these commands.

Operations on Text

In addition to math operations, Perl provides very powerful text manipulation functions. Much of this comes from Perl's background in UNIX system administration, where much of the data important to administrators lies in text files. Typically, each line in the text file is a record of information. The system password file (**/etc/passwd** or some variant) contains one line of text for each user. Each line is divided into fields (user name, real name, home directory for your account, and so on). Perl is very good at manipulating data files formatted like this.

The Difference Between Single and Double Quotes

Perl uses single or double quotes to indicate the start and end of text strings. This tells Perl where your Perl commands end and a string starts.

You can use either single or double quotes. Perl differentiates between strings surrounded by single or double quotes, ' or ". The difference is subtle.

Single Quotes

Single-quoted strings, such as 'hello world', are much more limited in scope than Perl's double-quoted strings, like "hello world". The reason is that Perl provides less interpretation of what's in a single-quoted string. In a single-quoted string:

- \n is two characters, a backslash and an *n*.
- \' (for an embedded single quote) and \\ (for an embedded back-slash) are the only allowed backslash escapes.

    You can have a real newline in the text, such as the following:

    ```
    'line 1
    line 2'
    ```

- The value of variables are not substituted, so that '$var' is simply a dollar sign and the letters *var*.

Double Quotes

Double-quoted strings provide more than single-quoted strings; for example:

- You can use the full set of backslash escapes, such as \t for a tab, \n for a newline, as listed in Table 2.5.
- You can substitute the value of variables, such as $var.
- You can also embed a newline in the string, the same as for single-quoted strings:

    ```
    "line 1
    line 2"
    ```

Table 2.5 Backslash escapes in Perl.

Perl	Usage
\\	Allow the use of a backslash.
\"	Double quote.
\a	Bell.
\b	Backspace.

\cN	Any control character (e.g., \cC for **Control-C**).
\e	The escape character (character 27).
\E	End a sequence of \L or \U.
\f	Formfeed.
\l	Make the next character lowercase.
\L	Make following characters lowercase until \E.
\n	Newline.
\r	Return.
\t	Tab.
\u	Make the next character uppercase.
\U	Make following characters uppercase until \E.
\0NN	Any octal numeric value.
\xNN	Any hexadecimal numeric value.

Thus, when you create your Perl scripts, it's important to use the quotes that you want and to know that there's a difference between ' and ". I stick to using doublequotes wherever possible, to avoid confusion.

Problems with Quotes

If your data already have quotes, you can use one of the odd q operators to create strings with quotes.

A single q creates a single-quoted string:

```
$var = q('Single-quoted string.');
print "$var\n";
```

This isn't very interesting, except that you can change the delimiters:

```
$var = q~String with "double" and 'single' quotes~;
print "$var\n";
# q.pl
```

The preceding example uses the tilde character, ~, as a replacement for the single-quote character. This allows your input data to contain single or double quotes.

The qq operator does the same for double-quoted strings:

```
# Example of the Q operator (see Star Trek).
# Double-quotes
$var = qq("Double-quoted string.");
print "$var\n";

$var = qq~String with "double" and 'single' quotes~;
print "$var\n";
# qq.pl
```

String Functions

Perl provides scads of string functions.

The length function returns the number of characters in a string:

```
$str_length = length($string);
```

For example:

```
# Determine string length.
$string = "This is a string";
$str_length = length($string);

print "The length of \"$string\" is $str_length.\n";
# length.pl
```

The chr function returns the character for a given numeric value, using US ASCII:

```
$letter = chr($value);
```

For example:

```
# Convert values to characters.
$letter = chr(69);
```

```
print "Letter is $letter.\n";
# chr.pl
```

Lowercase and Uppercase

You can convert a string from lowercase to uppercase with the uc function:

```
$lower = "all lowercase";
$upper = uc($lower);
print "$upper\n";
```

You can reverse this and convert a string to all lowercase with the lc function:

```
$upper = "ALL UPPERCASE";
$lower = lc($upper);
print "$lower\n";
```

If you work with multiple platforms, especially Windows and UNIX, you'll often need to convert file names from uppercase to lower, or vice versa.

WINDOWS

Case matters in UNIX, Windows 95, and Windows NT but not in Windows 3.1.

Searching in Strings

The index function returns the location of the first occurrence of a substring within a string:

```
$start = index($string, $look_for);
```

For example:

```
# Look for a substring with index.

$look_for = "then";
$start = index("First A, then B", $look_for);
```

```
print "$look_for starts at $start\n";
# index.pl
```

48

The variable $start gets the character position where the string "then" is located.

If you intend to search a string for multiple occurrences, you can use the optional start position:

```
$start = index($string, $look_for, $start_position);
```

You can search from the back of the string with rindex:

```
$start = rindex($string, $look_for);
$start = rindex($string, $look_for, $start_position);
```

You'll often use index and rindex with substr, which returns a substring from a string. Use index or rindex to find the start of the data you want and substr to extract it. The substr function takes the following parameters:

```
$new_string = substr($string, $offset, $length);
```

The substr function returns a new string, starting at $offset in $string, for $length characters. If you omit the $length, substr returns the substring from $offset to the end of the string.

The following example extracts the word *liberty* from the string "Give me liberty...", as shown in the **substr1.pl** script, which follows:

```
# Extract substring.

$string = "Give me liberty...";

$new_string = substr($string, 8, 7);

print "Substring is \"$new_string\".\n";

# substr1.pl
```

You can also go backwards with `substr`. If the offset is negative, `substr` counts from the end of the string. In the following example, the word *Three* is extracted from the end of the string:

```perl
# Extract sub-string.

$string = "One Two Three";

$new_string = substr($string, -5);

print "Sub-string is \"$new_string\".\n";

# substr2.pl
```

Perl provides many more string and text functions. See the online documentation on **perlfunc** for more. In addition, Chapter 3 covers Perl operations on files and processing text read in from files. Chapter 4 introduces using search patterns and regular expressions to parse the data read in from files.

String Operators

You can combine strings using Perl's string operators, as listed in Table 2.6.

Table 2.6 String operators.

Operator	Result
$s1 . $s2	Returns $s2 concatenated onto end of $s1.
$s1 x *value*	Returns $s1 repeated *value* times.
$s1 .= $s2	Appends $s2 onto end of $s1.

You can try the x times pattern using the following example:

```perl
#
# Repeat a string x times.
#
$s1 = "Value";
```

```
$s1 = $s1 x 10;

print "$s1\n";
```

```
# repeat.pl
```

Variables and Arrays

Perl variables allow you to store text, numbers, or lists of either. Perl attempts to hide any sort of limit, so string variables, for instance, can hold as much text as you can fit into your system's virtual memory. String variables simply grow as needed, as do all other Perl variables.

Perl's variables fall into three major types: scalars, arrays, and associative arrays. Perl differentiates variable names based on the first character $, @, or % respectively as shown in Table 2.7.

Table 2.7 How to differentiate variables in Perl.

Syntax	Meaning
NAME	File handle or directory handle, see Chapter 3.
$ *NAME*	A scalar variable.
@*NAME*	An array indexed by position number.
%*NAME*	An associative array indexed by string.
&*NAME*	Invoke the subroutine *NAME*.
*NAME	Everything named *NAME*.

Scalar Variables

Scalar variables hold a single value, either a text string or a number. You can set the same variable to hold either text or numeric data, and you can switch by setting a string variable to hold a number, and vice versa.

Arrays

In addition to scalar variables, Perl supports lists and arrays. A *list* is simply an ordered set of scalar values—text or numbers or both.

An *array* is a named list. When you use an array variable, you use the @ character, rather than the $, as in the following:

```
# Array example.
@array = (1,2,3,'red');
print "@array\n";

# array1.pl
```

When you run this script, you'll see the following output:

```
1 2 3 red
```

You can freely mix and match numbers and text in Perl lists and arrays.

The (1,2,3,'red') shows the syntax Perl uses to place data into a list. The preceding commands then set an array variable, @array, to the value of the list, which is all the elements in the list.

An empty list is represented as parenthesis with nothing in between:

```
() # Empty list.
```

Each element of an array is simply a scalar value, which you can access using the Perl syntax for scalars, $, with an index into the array. For example:

```
# Access
print "$array[1]\n";

# Assignment.
$array[2] = 'maroon';
```

Like C and C++, Perl starts counting array indices with 0. Thus, 1 represents the *second* element of the array.

N O T E

WARNING

Perl treats @array and $array as completely different values that have no relation to each other. This is even more confusing in that $array[value] refers to an element of @array, not to $array.

Because of this, I try to never use the same name in both scalar and array context.

You can place scalar variables in lists and arrays, as in the following example:

```
# A second array example.
$element = "Ouch";
@array = ($element, 1, 2, 3, 4);
print "@array\n";

# array2.pl
```

You can also use an odd syntax to set elements in a list to equal the corresponding elements of another list. This leads to some odd-looking but very useful Perl commands. For example:

```
# Third array example.
($one, $two, $three) = (1..3);
print "$one $two $three\n";

($array[0], $array[1], $array[2]) = (1,2,3,'red');
print "@array\n";

# array3.pl
```

To determine the number of elements in an array, use the $#array syntax, as shown here:

```
# Length of array.

@array = (1,2,3,4,5,6,7,8,9);

print "@array\n";

$number = $#array + 1;
```

```
print "Number elements: $number.\n";
```

```
# arraylen.pl
```

The value $#array is the last element. Since the elements go from 0 to $#array, the total is $#array plus 1.

NOTE

A Slice of Life

You can *slice* out part of an array, to make a sort of subarray, using the following syntax:

```
# Slicing an array.
@array = (1,2,3,'red');
```

```
# Get a slice of array.
@array[0,1,2] = ('green', 'blue', 'orange');
print "@array\n";
```

```
# slice.pl
```

Splice

The splice command allows you to *splice* an array. That is, splice allows you to replace existing elements in an array with new elements. The basic syntax follows:

```
splice(@array, $offset, $length, $replace1, $replace2, ...);
```

The splice function removes elements in @array from $offset onward, for $length elements. (If you omit the length, then splice removes all elements from $offset onward to the end.) If you provide replacement values, these are inserted starting at $offset, replacing the elements removed.

You do not need to replace the same number of elements you remove.

N O T E

Most of the parameters are optional.

Since the use of `splice` tends to be obscure, a few examples might help.

```perl
# Use of splice on arrays.

@array = (1,2,3,4,5,6,7,8,9);

print "@array\n";

# Remove elements from position 7 onward.

$offset = 7;
splice(@array, $offset);
print "@array\n";

# Remove first element only and save it.
$offset = 0;  # first element
$length = 1;
($first) = splice(@array, $offset, $length);
print "@array\n";
print "First element: $first\n";

# Replace the second and third elements.
$offset = 1;
$length = 2; # two elements.
splice(@array, $offset, $length, 99, 98, 97, 96);
print "@array\n";

# splice.pl
```

When you run this script, you'll see the following transformations to `@array`:

```
1 2 3 4 5 6 7 8 9
1 2 3 4 5 6 7
2 3 4 5 6 7
First element: 1
2 99 98 97 96 5 6 7
```

Splice returns the elements it removes. You can store these data in variables, if you desire, as shown in the **splice.pl** script.

Other Array Commands

The reverse command reverses the order of the elements in a list, returning the new list. For example:

```
# Reverses elements in an array.
@array = (1,2,3,'red');
print "Before: @array\n";

@array = reverse(@array);
print "After: @array\n";

# reverse.pl
```

The sort command sorts an array:

```
# Sorts elements in an array.

@array = ('red', 'green', 'blue', 'orange', 'maroon');
print "Before: @array\n";

@sorted = sort(@array);
print "After: @sorted\n";

# sort.pl
```

There's more to sort, including the ability to pass your own subroutine to do the sorting. See the online documentation for more on this command.

Associative Arrays

One of the most interesting developments in Perl is associative arrays. The regular arrays, which we have already covered, allow you to access elements by their index numbers, starting at zero. Associative arrays, on the other hand allow you to access elements by key names. That is, an associative array holds a set of key/value pairs.

A *key name* is any arbitrary scalar value, such as "HOME", "USER-NAME", or anything else you care to use.

Associative arrays are very useful for storing the attributes of an item, especially when you don't know in advance how many attributes an item will have. For example, if a user can customize an application, some attributes to store might be foreground color, background color, font name, starting directory, and directory path to system files. The user may customize any, all, or none of these attributes. Such tasks are great for associative arrays.

Perl uses a percent sign, %, to indicate a variable is an associative array. Thus, %assoc represents a variable named *assoc* that is an associative array.

To access individual values in an associative array, you use a different syntax. Any value in an associative array can be accessed through its key name, using the following syntax:

```
%assoc{keyname}
```

For example:

```
# Associative arrays.
$assoc{"Name"} = "Grover Cleveland";
$assoc{23} = 365;
$assoc{123.45} = "Hello world";

$key = 123.45;
print "Element 123.45: $assoc{$key}\n";
$key = "Name";
print "Element Name: $assoc{$key}\n";

#assoc1.pl
```

As you can see, any scalar value is acceptable as a key name.

As with arrays, %array, $array and @array all refer to *different* variables, so watch out.

WARNING

An associative array has no particular value itself, so trying to print an associative array won't do you much good. In addition, Perl stores associative arrays in any order it desires (presumably an order that allows Perl the most efficient access to the array elements). So, if you have an associative array and don't know everything in the array, how do you extract the values? For this, Perl provides the keys operator.

The keys operator returns a list of all the key names within an associative array. You can then go through this list to extract all the key names, as shown next:

```
# Associative array keys.

$assoc{"Name"} = "Grover Cleveland";
$assoc{"Address"} = "1600 Penn.";
$assoc{"City"} = "Washington";

@key_names = keys(%assoc);

print "Key names are: @key_names\n\n";

# Now, access each element from the list.

foreach $key (@key_names) {

    print "$key holds $assoc{$key}\n";
}

# keys.pl
```

When you run the **keys.pl** script, the order of the keys will probably not be the order in which you entered the values.

Similar to the keys operator, the values operator allows you to extract all the values of an associative array, in the same order that keys returns the key names, as shown here:

```
# Associative array values.

$assoc{"Name"} = "Grover Cleveland";
$assoc{"Address"} = "1600 Penn.";
$assoc{"City"} = "Washington";

@values = values(%assoc);

print "Values are: @values\n\n";

# values.pl
```

Since all the values in an associative array are stored as key/value pairs, you can use the each operator to extract a key/value pair as a list from the array, for each element. For example:

```
# Associative array access with each.

$assoc{"Name"} = "Grover Cleveland";
$assoc{"Address"} = "1600 Penn.";
$assoc{"City"} = "Washington";

# Access each element with each.

while ( ($key,$value) = each(%assoc) ) {
    print "Key: $key \t Value: $value\n";
}

# each.pl
```

In the **each.pl** script, the list returned by the each operator is separated into individual scalar variables $key and $value. You could instead use the list returned by each as a list, should you desire.

In addition to each, you can assign a whole associative array to a normal array to get a list of all key/value pairs, as shown next:

```
# Associative array to normal array.

$assoc{"Name"} = "Grover Cleveland";
$assoc{"Address"} = "1600 Penn.";
$assoc{"City"} = "Washington";

@array = %assoc;

print "As array: @array\n";

# assoc2.pl
```

The delete operator removes a key/value pair from an associative array. To use delete, you need to delete the value. For example:

```
# Deleting associative array elements.

$assoc{"Name"} = "Grover Cleveland";
$assoc{"Address"} = "1600 Penn.";
$assoc{"City"} = "Washington";

# Print keys before.
@key_names = keys(%assoc);

print "Key names are: @key_names\n\n";

delete $assoc{"Address"};

# Print keys after .
@key_names = keys(%assoc);

print "Key names now: @key_names\n\n";

# delete.pl
```

To tell if a given key name exists in an associative array, you can use the `exists` operator:

```
if ( exists($assoc{$key} ) ) {

    # ..
}
```

The Environment Associative Array

One of the most useful associative arrays is %ENV, which holds your system's environment variables. These variables, supported on UNIX and Windows, provide a number of values set up by the user (or for the user) that pertain to the computer's environment. On UNIX, for example, the SHELL environment variable holds the user's desired command-entry shell program, such as **/bin/csh** for the C shell.

Using the `keys` operator, you can easily access the %ENV associative array and see what's available on the system. Enter the following script and try it out on your system:

```
# Access environment variables.

@key_names = keys(%ENV);

print "Key names are: @key_names\n\n";

# Now, access each element from the list.

foreach $key (@key_names) {

    print "$key=$ENV{$key}\n";
}
# env.pl
```

On a Linux system, you'll see a lot of output, including the following output, which has been edited for space:

```
HOSTTYPE=i486-linux
LOGNAME=erc
OSTYPE=linux
WINDOWID=29360141
SHLVL=1
OPENWINHOME=/usr/openwin
MANPATH=/usr/local/man:/usr/man/preformat:/usr/man:/usr/X11/man:/usr/open
win/man
LESSOPEN=|lesspipe.sh %s
HOME=/home/erc
PWD=/home/erc/perl/book/scripts
DISPLAY=:0.0
LESS=-MM
SHELL=/bin/csh
TERM=xterm
MACHTYPE=i386
HOST=yonsen
ignoreeof=10
HOSTNAME=yonsen.yonsen.org
USER=erc
```

On a Windows 95 system, you'll see something like:

```
WINBOOTDIR=C:\WINDOWS
TMP=C:\WINDOWS\TEMP
PROMPT=$p$g
TEMP=C:\DOS
SOUND=C:\MOZART
COMSPEC=C:\WINDOWS\COMMAND.COM
CMDLINE=perl env.pl
BLASTER=A220 I5 D1 T4
PATH=C:\WINDOWS;C:\WINDOWS\COMMAND;C:\DOS;C:\PERL\BIN;
WINDIR=C:\WINDOWS
```

On Windows NT, you'll see a lot more useful values:

```
USERNAME=erc
PROMPT=$P$G
```

```
PROCESSOR_IDENTIFIER=x86 Family 5 Model 2 Stepping 11, GenuineIntel
PROCESSOR_ARCHITECTURE=x86
OS=Windows_NT
HOME=C:/users/default
ComSpec=C:\WINNT35.0\system32\cmd.exe
windir=C:\WINNT35.0
Path=.;C:\perl\bin;c:\mksnt\mksnt;C:\WINNT35.0\system32;C:\WINNT35.0;c:\l
ocal\bin;c:\msvc20\bin
temp=C:\temp
PROCESSOR_LEVEL=5
Os2LibPath=C:\WINNT35.0\system32\os2\dll;
HOMEDRIVE=c:
ROOTDIR=c:/mksnt
include=c:\msvc20\include;c:\msvc20\include\gl;%include%
CPU=i386
SystemRoot=C:\WINNT35.0
PROCESSOR_REVISION=020b
TMPDIR=C:/temp
COMPUTERNAME=YONSEN
tmp=C:\temp
HOMEPATH=\users\johnsone
LIB=c:\msvc20\lib
SystemDrive=C:
```

Notice that both Windows NT and UNIX systems tend to have similar environment variables, such as HOME. NT sports a USERNAME environment variable, while UNIX tends to use USER.

Built-In Variables

Perl provides a huge number of built-in variables, most with very bizarre syntax, such as $_, the default input and pattern-matching variable.

The reason for variables like $_ is to allow you to write minimalist Perl scripts, like the following **minimal.pl** script:

```
#
# minimal.pl
# One of the most minimal scripts
```

```
# in perl, using $_ to effect.
#
# This script prints out all
# files listed on the command line.
#
while (<>) {      # From <ARGV>
    print;  # Prints $_
}
```

The **minimal.pl** script opens each file in turn, since <> is a shorthand for <ARGV>, which is a shorthand for treating each command-line argument as a file name. When the file is open, it reads the contents of the file.

By default, print prints out the hidden variable $_. You'll almost always want to avoid $_ and specify the data to print directly, because using hidden variables tends to make your Perl scripts harder to understand. The preceding script showed Perl's roots in awk and the system administration community. You can write very small minimalist Perl scripts that do a lot; however, it's rather hard to tell what the script is supposed to do, as illustrated in **minimal.pl**, unless you're a Perl expert.

A more expanded version of the minimal script follows:

```
#
# minimal2.pl
# A slightly longer minimalist perl script.
#
# This script prints out all
# files listed on the command line.
#
while (<ARGV>) {
    print $_;
}
```

The preceding script clearly points where the data are coming from, but still doesn't show how the files are being opened and read. See Chapter 3 for more on files.

Command-Line Arguments

The preceding minimalist Perl script introduced the concept of ARGV, which should look familiar to C programmers. ARGV in Perl represents the command-line arguments, those extra values you place on the command line. You can use ARGV in different ways.

<ARGV> represents opening each file that is listed by name on the command line. @ARGV is a Perl array that contains each of the command-line arguments as a separate array element.

The following code shows how to extract each command-line argument, one at a time. You can use the array $ARGV[element] syntax, if you want, or you can use shift:

```
# Lists command-line arguments.

# Get first argument.
$arg = shift(@ARGV);

# Loop while there is an argument.
while ($arg) {
    print "$arg\n";

    # Get next argument.
    $arg = shift(@ARGV);
}
# listargs.pl
```

The shift operator extracts the first element of an array, shortening the array in the process.

The opposite of shift is unshift, which prepends data onto the front of an array. The unshift command prepends data onto an array:

```
$num_elements = unshift(array, $prepend_data);
```

For example:

```
$prepend_data = "PREPENDED";
$num_elements = unshift(@ARGV, $prepend_data);
```

You can try this with your command-line arguments, using the following example:

```
# Uses unshift with ARGV.
$prepend_data = "PREPENDED";
$num_elements = unshift(@ARGV, $prepend_data);

# Display arguments.
foreach $i (0 .. $#ARGV) {
    print "$ARGV[$i]\n";
}

# unshift.pl
```

The **unshift.pl** script uses a different method to iterate through the list of command-line arguments. With Perl, there's usually more than one way to get the job done. The variable $#ARGV contains the number of elements in @ARGV.

To test this script, you then need to pass some command-line arguments to the **unshift.pl** script. For example:

```
perl unsift.pl u*
```

You'll see output like the following:

```
PREPENDED
unsift.pl
until1.pl
upper.pl
```

Notice how the word *PREPENDED* gets prepended onto ARGV by the unshift command.

Now that you've seen @ARGV and %ENV, Table 2.8 lists a number of the special global variables in Perl.

Table 2.8 Some special global variables in Perl.

Variable	Usage
$_	Default input and pattern-searching variable.
$0	Contains the name of the Perl script being executed.
@ARGV	Array containing all command-line parameters.
$#ARGV	Index of last elements in @ARGV.
%ENV	Associative array containing all environment variables.

Subroutines

So far, all the Perl scripts simply execute from top to bottom. This works rather well for the simple scripts used to illustrate points. But, when the time comes for you to write sophisticated Perl scripts, you'll probably want to use subroutines extensively.

A *subroutine* is a named section of Perl code that you can call to execute special commands. Normally, you'll use subroutines as a way to better organize your Perl scripts. In addition, subroutines are great for developing a set of Perl code to share with your other Perl scripts. (You can collect such subroutines together into Perl packages. See Chapter 7 for more on this topic.)

You define subroutines with the sub statement:

```
# First subroutine.

sub my_subroutine {

    print "In a subroutine.\n";
```

```
}

# Invoke the subroutine
print "Before subroutine.\n";

&my_subroutine;

print "After subroutine.\n";

# sub1.pl
```

The sub statement defines a block, from { to }, that is your subroutine. Each subroutine requires a name, given by you (my_subroutine in the preceding **sub1.pl** example).

The Perl commands defined in the sub block don't execute right away. Instead, you need to use the &subroutine_name syntax to invoke, or execute, the subroutine at the place or places you want. You can invoke subroutines as many times as you'd like.

Returning Data From Subroutines

Subroutines return the value of the last expression evaluated. So, to return a particular value, you can place that value in a statement of its own. As long as this is the last statement executed in the subroutine, that's the value returned. Or, you can use the return statement. I tend to use return, since it more clearly shows the value returned from the subroutine.

For example, the following script returns a scalar value from a subroutine:

```
# Returning data from subroutines.

$value = &two;
print "Two is $value.\n";

#
# You can define subroutines above
# or below or in between the main
# Perl statements.
#
```

```
sub two {

    return 2;

}
```

```
# sub2.pl
```

Chances are your scripts won't be so simple.

Accessing Variables in Subroutines

In your subroutines, you can access the value of any global variable, and all variables used so far have been global. This means that a subroutine can use data set up by other parts of your Perl scripts, as shown in the following **sub3.pl** script:

```
# Accessing global variables in subroutines.

$a = 1;
$b = 4;

$value = &add;

print "$a plus $b is $value.\n";

sub add {

    return ($a + $b);
}
# sub3.pl
```

The add subroutine adds the values of $a and $b, based on whatever data you place in $a and $b.

WARNING

You have to be careful when accessing global variables in subroutines that you have properly set up the values before calling the subroutine.

Local Variables in Subroutines

Because all the variables we've used so far are global variables, using subroutines introduces a new problem—unintentionally overwriting variables. If your subroutine uses variables, you may accidentally name these variables the same as other variables used in your Perl script. Thus, the values won't be what you expect. Such problems also tend to be very difficult to track down.

To help combat this problem, Perl allows you to create *local variables* inside subroutines. These local variables may be named the same as any global variables, but because they are local, you won't overwrite the global variables.

To make a variable local, use the my command (as in my variable), as shown next:

```
# Local variables in subroutines.

$a = 1;
$b = 4;

# sum is global.
$sum = 10;

$value = &add;

print "$a plus $b is $value.\n";
print "Global sum remains $sum.\n";

sub add {
```

```
# This sum is local.
my($sum) = $a + $b;

print "Local sum=$sum.\n";
return $sum;
}
```

```
# sub4.pl
```

In the **sub4.pl** script, the variable $sum is used as a global variable as well as a local variable. The *sum* inside the add subroutine is not the same as the *sum* used previously in global context. The use of my protects your subroutine from unanticipated side effects.

N O T E   Older versions of Perl supported only the local command instead of my. For most usage, you can use local or my interchangeably; however, using my makes your programs slightly more efficient. Furthermore, if you write modules (see chapter 7), you'll need to use my instead of local.

There's one case where you need to use local instead of my, which is covered in the following **sub8.pl script**.

Passing Parameters to Subroutines

Most computer languages allow you to pass parameters to subroutines, and Perl does, too, although in a manner that evokes ancient history in computing. Instead of directly specifying the parameters inside a subroutine, Perl places all the parameters into an array named @_.

You can access this array directly, with the @_ syntax, or access individual parameters, such as $_[0] for the first parameter, $_[1] for the second, and so on. In most cases, you'll want to place subroutine parameters into local variables.

In the example script **sub5.pl**, which follows, we extend the add subroutine to make it even more general purpose, by passing parameters to add. By using parameters, we don't have to set up the global variables $a and $b and, therefore, are free from extra worry about how the subroutine works. Instead, we just pass the two parameters to add as shown here:

```
# Parameters to subroutines.

$value = &add(5, 6);
print "Value from add=$value.\n";

$value = &add(25, 1);
print "Value from add=$value.\n";

#
# This subroutine adds the two parameters
# passed to it. It is more general than
# the ones before, which depended on the
# values of global variables $a and $b.
#
sub add {

    my($a, $b) = @_;

    my($sum) = $a + $b;

    return $sum;
}

# sub5.pl
```

The **sub5.pl** script uses the parameter array, **@_**, as an array. You can also access individual elements of the array, as shown next:

```
# Parameters to subroutines.

$value = &add(5, 6);
print "Value from add=$value.\n";

$value = &add(25, 1);
print "Value from add=$value.\n";

#
# This subroutine adds the two parameters
```

```
# passed to it. It is more general than
# the ones before, which depended on the
# values of global variables $a and $b.
#
sub add {

    my($a) = $_[0];  # First parameter.
    my($b) = $_[1];  # Second parameter.

    my($sum) = $a + $b;

    return $sum;
}

# sub6.pl
```

The results of both **sub5.pl** and **sub6.pl** should be the same.

NOTE With Perl 5, you can omit the leading ampersand, &, on subroutine calls if you use parenthesis for the list of parameters. For example, instead of:

```
$value = &add(5, 6);
```

you can omit the ampersand, as shown here:

```
$value = add(5, 6);
```

You can also omit the ampersand if the subroutine is declared before its use.

Changing the Value of Subroutine Parameters

Up to now, the subroutines have taken in data and returned data. Beyond that, you'll often want to change the values of the input parameters.

For scalar values, you can set a new value into the @_ array, for example:

```
# Modifies parameters in subroutine.

$one  = 1;
$two  = 2;
```

```
$three = 3;

print "Before: $one, $two, $three.\n";
&increment($one, $two, $three);

print "After: $one, $two, $three.\n";

#
# Subroutine: increments each
# parameter passed to it.
#
sub increment {

    # Increment each parameter.
    for ($i = 0; $i <= $#_; $i++) {
        $_[$i] += 1;
    }
}

# sub7.pl
```

WARNING

This method works only for scalar values.

In the **sub7.pl** script, the increment subroutine handles any number of parameters you choose to pass to it, incrementing each by using the $#_ variable, which represents the index of the last element in the array @_. (You soon get used to typing punctuation with Perl.)

If you want to pass in an array, for instance, and then have the subroutine modify the global array, you need to use the special * syntax. The *name construct refers to all instances of name, such as $name, @name, and %name. You can use this to alias a local variable in a subroutine to a passed in array.

Using this method, you must use local, not my, to declare the variable local in the subroutine.

N O T E

In the following example, the @array gets passed to the subroutine mod_array. Inside mod_array, the local variable local_array gets aliased to the global @array. (Actually, the * causes @local_array to be aliased to @array, as well as $local_array to $array and %local_array to %array, should these exist as well. In this example, only @array is used for all the aliases.)

The **sub8.pl** script follows:

```
# Passing an array and modifying it.

@array = (1,2,3,4,5,6,7,8,9);

print "Before: @array.\n";

&mod_array( *array );

print "After: @array.\n";

sub mod_array {

    # Alias local_array to passed in array.
    local(*local_array) = @_;

    @local_array = reverse(@local_array);
}

# sub8.pl
```

It's hard to keep track of "those funny symbols," as Larry Wall, the creator of Perl puts it. Table 2.9 lists Larry's definitions for $, @, and all the other funny symbols.

Table 2.9 Those funny symbols.

Symbol	Can Be Read As
$	the
@	those
%	relationship
&	do
*	any sort of

Summary

Perl provides more than the full standard set of commands to control the flow of your scripts, from `if` to `while` to `for` to `foreach`. In addition, Perl provides a set of tricky control statements, such as `unless`. There's a lot of flexibility and freedom in Perl.

Along with the control statements, Perl provides a huge set of functions, such as `substr`, that you can call to convert data and perform various tasks. The online documentation on **Perlfunc** lists them in Perlish detail.

Array variables in Perl use a leading @, rather than the leading $ for scalar values. An array is simply a named list of values.

An associative array allows you to place values in the array along with key names. Access is then through the key names. For associative array variables, use a leading % rather than @ or $.

Subroutines allow you to share code and compartmentalize your work. Unfortunately, Perl uses a bizarre method to pass parameters to subroutines, adding to the complexity of Perl scripts.

That's a lot of Perl. You've now been exposed to the major syntax required by Perl and should be ready to start writing Perl scripts that interact with your system. One of the most frequently used ways to do that is to read and write files, the topic of Chapter 3.

Perl Commands Introduced in This Chapter

```
chr
continue
delete
do
each
exists
for
foreach
goto
index
keys
last
lc
length
local
my
next
q
qq
redo
return
reverse
rindex
shift
sort
splice
sub
substr
uc
unless
unshift
until
values
while
```

Working with Files

This chapter covers:

- Opening files
- Reading data from files
- Closing files
- Windows and UNIX file-naming conventions
- Using die to react to errors
- Reading the file names within a directory
- Manipulating files in a directory
- Getting information on files
- Copying files

Files

Chances are good that, if you're working with Perl, you also need to work with files. The files may contain data extracted from a database, source code that needs to be compiled, reports on system functions, or information used to generate a Web page. This chapter addresses this basic need by covering Perl's commands for file and directory access.

The most basic needs are opening files, reading the contents, and writing results.

Opening Files and File Handles

Before you can do much with a file's contents, you need to open the file with the open command, which was briefly introduced in Chapter 1:

```
open(filehandle, name);
```

The *file handle* is any name you provide, such as INPUT or OUTPUT. By convention, file handles use uppercase names. The file handle is merely a "handle" or means to refer to the open file.

Table 3.1 lists the special codes that go along with the file names and determine whether the file will open for reading or writing.

Table 3.1 File open codes.

File Name	Meaning
<filename	Open file for input.
+<filename	Open file for input and output.
+>filename	Open file for input and output, truncate existing data.
filename	Open file for input.
>filename	Open file for output, truncate existing data.
>>filename	Open file for output, append to end of existing data.

WINDOWS

Windows and UNIX use different file-naming conventions. UNIX separates directory names with a forward slash, /, and Windows uses a backward slash, \. To add to the confusion, the backward slash is an escape character in Perl, so you need to supply two backward slashes, or \\, to signify the Windows directory separator to Perl.

In addition, the MS-DOS or FAT file system places severe restrictions on file names. File names are not case-sensitive. The base part of the file name can be only eight characters long. An extension is allowed with up to three characters after a period. This is the only period character allowed in file names. The Windows NT file system, or NTFS, allows for longer names.

Windows 95 uses the FAT file system but gets around the restrictions on file name length by encoding a longer name within the file header. Under Windows 95 (and NT 4.0), you can have file names with spaces in them, something that Perl, with its UNIX roots, will have a hard time dealing with.

When you're done with a file, call `close`:

```
close(filehandle);
```

Or Else, Die!

If `open` fails to open the file, your Perl script is in trouble. The most common way to deal with this is to use the Perl `or  die` syntax to call `die`, which prints out a message and exits your script. For example:

```
open(INPUT, $input) or
    die "Can't open $input.";
```

N O T E If you place a newline in the message passed to `die`, then `die` will only print your message before exiting. If you omit the newline, `die` will print extra information including the file and line number where the problem occurred. Since this extra information is very useful, I normally leave off the newline when calling `die`.

You can use the Perl `or` syntax to cause a fatal error if a file can't be opened.

For example, to copy the contents of one file into another (assuming both files are text files and the source file already exists), you can use the following code:

```
#
# copy1.pl
#
# Build up file names from
# command-line arguments.
#
# Usage:
```

```
#    copy1.pl infile outfile
#
$input = $ARGV[0];
$output = ">" . $ARGV[1];

open(INPUT, $input) or die "Can't open $input.";
open(OUTPUT, $output)
    or die "Can't open $output.";

# Use shorthand for reading file.
while (<INPUT>) {
    print OUTPUT $_;
}

close (INPUT);
close (OUTPUT);


# copy1.pl
```

This Perl script takes $ARGV[0], the first command-line argument, as an input file name and copies the file to $ARGV[1], the second command-line argument, which names the output file.

WINDOWS

MS-DOS, the predecessor to Windows, supports the concept of binary and textual file access. In text mode, trailing carriage return/newline characters are often converted to a single newline character. The purpose is to help map between various operating system text file formats. (Windows uses carriage return-newline at the end of each line of text, UNIX uses a newline only, and the Macintosh uses a carriage return only.)

This creates a problem with binary files. Any sequence of 13–10 will get mapped to a 10, and this may well damage your data. If you have a binary file, then you want to use the binmode command:

```
binmode(filehandle);
```

The binmode command sets up a file for access in binary mode with no mapping of carriage returns.

Reading Files

In addition to the shorthand method for reading in a file, Perl provides a number of functions to read data from a file. You can use the method presented in the **asklang.pl** script in Chapter 1:

```
$lang = <STDIN>;
```

This command reads one line from the file handle STDIN. You can use any file handle opened for input in place of STDIN.

In addition to this method, the read function reads a number of bytes from a file:

```
$bytes_read = read(filehandle, $var, $length, $offset);
```

The read function reads $length number of bytes (or tries to), placing the data into $var. If you provide the optional $offset, the read takes place starting at that location in the file. The read function returns the number of bytes it actually read, which alerts you to errors, especially if the result is < 0.

```
#
# read.pl
#
# Use read command to read data from a file
# and copy file to output file.
#
# Usage:
#     read.pl infile outfile
#
$input = $ARGV[0];
$output = ">" . $ARGV[1];

open(INPUT, $input) ||
    die "Can't open $input.";
open(OUTPUT, $output) ||
    die "Can't open $output.";
```

```
# You can experiment with different buffer sizes.
$length = 1024;

$bytes_read = read(INPUT, $var, $length);

while ($bytes_read > 0) {
    print OUTPUT $var;

    # Read next block of data.
    $bytes_read = read(INPUT, $var, $length);
}

close (INPUT);
close (OUTPUT);

# read.pl
```

Like the preceding **copy1.pl** script, this Perl script takes $ARGV[0], the first command-line argument, as an input file name and copies the file to $ARGV[1], the second command-line argument, which names the output file.

Instead of using the shorthand <INPUT> method of reading in the file one line at a time, this function uses read and a buffer size ($length) of 1024 bytes.

Similar to read, the getc function reads one character from a file:

```
$char = getc(filehandle);
```

 The getc command is not very efficient. You should use read instead.

N O T E

The eof function returns true if the file is positioned at the end. *EOF* is short for endoffile.

```
if (eof(filehandle) ) {

    # Handle end-of-file condition...
}
```

Normally, read and getc are set up to read sequentially from the beginning of a file to the end. If you need to access a particular location within a file, you can use seek.

```
seek(filehandle, $position, $whence);
```

Seek moves the file position to the value you provide. The $whence specifies where to start, as listed in Table 3.2.

Table 3.2 Whence positions for seek.

Value	Meaning	UNIX
0	Set place in file $position bytes from start of file.	SEEK_SET
1	Set place to current position plus $position.	SEEK_CUR
2	Set place to the end of the file plus $position.	SEEK_END

The *UNIX* value in Table 3.2 refers to the UNIX/Posix C function fseek().

If you use a value of 2 for $whence, you normally set $position to a negative value, to move back from the end of the file. On most systems, moving beyond the end of the file will generate an error.

In connection with seek, the tell function returns the byte offset position you're at within a file:

```
$position = tell(filehandle);
```

The value returned by `tell` is the file pointer position, the number of bytes from the beginning, that the file pointer is located.

Writing Files

The `print` function introduced in Chapter 1 allows you to write data to a file.

 There's also a function called `write`, but it is not the opposite of `read`. Instead, Perl uses `write` to print formatted data for reports, as described in Chapter 5.

N O T E

The form of `print` to write to a file is:

```
print filehandle data_to_print;
```

Directories

In addition to accessing individual files, you'll also want to manipulate directories, list the contents of directories, and modify files inside the directories.

Reading the Contents of a Directory

The most common need with directories is listing the contents. To do so with Perl, you need to open the directory, read the elements, and then close the directory.

To open a directory, use the `opendir` command:

```
$status = opendir(dirhandle, $name);
```

To read a directory entry (usually a file name), use `readdir`:

```
$entry = readdir(dirhandle);
```

The `$entry` variable will then hold the file name read from the directory.

In scalar context, `readdir` returns the next entry. In array context, it returns all the contents of the directory, which is usually more efficient.

N O T E

If for some reason you've gone too far when processing directory and need to restart the listing from the beginning, you can rewind the directory handle back to the top with `rewinddir`:

```
rewinddir(dirhandle);
```

Finally, when you're done with a directory, you need to close it with `closedir`:

```
closedir(dirhandle);
```

Putting this all together, you can read all the entries in a directory with the following Perl code:

```
#
# Reads contents of a directory
# in scalar context (item by item).
#
# Usage:
#    readdir1.pl directory_name
#
$name = $ARGV[0];

opendir(DIR, $name) || die "Can't open $name";

$entry = readdir(DIR);

while (length($entry) > 0) {

    print "$entry\n";

    $entry = readdir(DIR);
}
```

```
closedir(DIR);
```

```
# readdir1.pl
```

The **readdir1.pl** script opens the directory named in the first command-line argument.

Using an array with `readdir`, instead of a scalar variable, your code looks a bit different:

```
#
# Reads contents of a directory
# in array context.
#
# Usage:
#    readdir2.pl directory_name
#
$name = $ARGV[0];

opendir(DIR, $name) || die "Can't open $name";

@entries = readdir(DIR);

closedir(DIR);

  # Sort results.
@sorted = sort(@entries);

foreach $entry (@sorted) {
    print "$entry\n";
}
```

```
# readdir2.pl
```

Since `readdir` returns the entire list in array context, you can then easily sort the list with `sort`.

To create a directory, use `mkdir`:

```
mkdir($directory_name, $mode);
```

The $mode is a numeric set of UNIX read, write, and execute permissions, which is masked by your default umask value. Table 3.3 lists the UNIX permission values used for the $mode.

Table 3.3 UNIX file permissions.

Value	Meaning
0400	Owner of file has read permission.
0200	Owner has write permission.
0100	Owner has execute permission.
0040	All users in same group have read permission.
0020	Group users have write permission.
0010	Group users have execute permission.
0004	All users have read permission.
0002	All users have write permission.
0001	All users have execute permission.

You add up all the permissions. For example, 0666 means all users can read and write.

 While you may think this is proof that Perl is possessed, the value actually comes from UNIX. See Appendix A for a listing of UNIX books that cover file permissions, and the **chmod**, **mkdir**, and **umask** commands.

NOTE

The umask value is then subtracted from 0777 (all users can do everything). For example, a umask of 0007 would make your default protection mask 0770 (determined by subtracting 0007 from 0777).

To remove a directory, use rmdir:

```
rmdir($directory_name);
```

To change to a different working directory, use chdir:

```
chdir($directory_name);
```

Globbing Around: An easier way to read the contents of a directory is often to change to that directory and then use glob:

N O T E @list = glob(expression);

The expression needs to be a shell-style wildcard, such as *.pl* for all file names ending in *.pl*. If you use glob, you'll normally want to change to the directory first, with chdir, as described previously.

```
#
# Uses glob to read all .pl
# files in current directory.
#

@list = glob("\*.pl");

print ".pl files: @list\n";

# glob.pl
```

Getting Information on a File

The stat function gets a host of information about a file:

```
($dev, $inode, $mode, $nlink,
 $uid, $gid, $rdev, $size, $atime,
 $mtime, $ctime, $blksize, $blocks) = stat(file);
```

The *file* can be either a file handle referring to a file you've opened or a file name.

The values returned are listed in Table 3.4.

Table 3.4 The data returned from stat.

Value	Holds
$dev	Device number of file system.
$inode	Inode number.

$mode	File mode (type and permissions).
$nlink	Number of hard links to the file.
$uid	Numeric user ID of file's owner.
$gid	Numeric group ID of file's owner.
$rdev	The device identifier device (special) files only.
$size	Total size of file, in bytes.
$atime	Time of last access.
$mtime	Time of last modification.
$ctime	Time of inode change.
$blksize	Preferred block size for file system I/O.
$blocks	Actual number of blocks allocated.

In addition to stat, there's a similar function called lstat, which provides information on a symbolic link.

If the information in Table 3.4 seems overly detailed, chances are you will never use stat. However, you may want to use one of the more convenient file tests.

The following script takes a directory name from the command line and runs stat on each of the entries within the directory:

```
#
# Lists files in directory; then
# gets info on files with stat.
#
# Usage:
#    stat.pl directory_name
#
$name = $ARGV[0];

opendir(DIR, $name) ||
    die "Can't open $name";

@entries = readdir(DIR);

closedir(DIR);
```

```perl
    # Sort results.
@sorted = sort(@entries);

foreach $entry (@sorted) {

    # Test each file.
    print "\n\nFile $entry\n";

    ($dev, $inode, $mode, $nlink,
     $uid, $gid, $rdev, $size, $atime,
     $mtime, $ctime, $blksize, $blocks) = stat($entry);

    print "Device number    : $dev\n";
    print "Inode number     : $inode\n";
    print "File mode        : $mode\n";
    print "Number hard links: $nlink\n";
    print "Owner ID         : $uid\n";
    print "Owner Group ID   : $gid\n";
    print "Device ID        : $rdev\n";
    print "Total size       : $size\n";
    print "Last access time : $atime\n";
    print "Last modify time : $mtime\n";
    print "Last inode time  : $ctime\n";
    print "Block size       : $blksize\n";
    print "Number blocks    : $blocks\n";
}


# stat.pl
```

If you don't have permission to read the file, lstat and stat will return nothing.

Since stat and lstat come from UNIX, you may have problems on Windows, especially Windows 95. Oftentimes, you'll have problems running stat on a top-level directory.

Testing Files

Much like UNIX shell scripts, you can test files (or potential files) to see if they exist, can be written to, and so on.

Each of the commands in Table 3.5 take either a file name (as a string) or a file handle.

Table 3.5 File test commands.

Command	Returns
-r filehandle	True if readable.
-w filehandle	True if writable.
-x filehandle	True if executable.
-z filehandle	True if file exists and has zero size.
-s filehandle	Returns size if file exists and has nonzero size.
-e filehandle	True if file exists.
-f filehandle	True if file is a normal file.
-d filehandle	True if file is a directory.
-l filehandle	True if file is a symbolic link.
-S filehandle	True if file is a socket (uppercase *S*).
-p filehandle	True if file is a named pipe (FIFO).

While more convenient that calling `stat`, the syntax for these tests looks odd unless you're used to UNIX shell scripting. To test if a named file is readable, you'd use code like the following:

```
if (-r $filename) {
    # Is readable...
}
```

For example, to read all the entries in a directory and print out data on the files, you can use the following script:

```
#
# Lists files in directory; then
# tests files for data.
#
# Usage:
#    filetest.pl directory_name
#
$name = $ARGV[0];

opendir(DIR, $name) || die "Can't open $name";

@entries = readdir(DIR);

closedir(DIR);

  # Sort results.
@sorted = sort(@entries);

foreach $entry (@sorted) {

    # Test each file.
    print "$entry    ";

    if (-r $entry) {
        print "r";
    } else {
        print "-";
    }

    if (-w $entry) {
        print "w";
    } else {
        print "-";
    }

    if (-x $entry) {
        print "x";
    } else {
```

```
        print "-";
    }


    $size = -s $entry;
    print " $size bytes, ";

    if (-d $entry) {
        print "directory ";
    } elsif (-f $entry) {
        print "normal file ";
    } elsif (-l $entry) {
        print "symbolic link ";
    } elsif (-p $entry) {
        print "FIFO pipe ";
    } else {
        print "Unknown file type.\n";
    }

    print "\n"; # End line.
}


# filetest.pl
```

WINDOWS

Many of these tests are problematic on Windows.

There are more tests than the ones shown in Table 3.5, but they tend to be obscure. See the online documentation for more information.

Manipulating Files in a Directory

The chmod command allows you to modify the read, write, and execute permissions on a file. In UNIX, for example, only files marked with the execute permission can be executed.

The chmod command takes the following parameters:

```
chmod($mode, $filename);
```

You can pass more than one file name. The $mode is a numeric value based on UNIX file permissions and is usually specified in octal notation. To mark a file as read-only, you can use the following command:

```
chmod(0444, $filename);
```

See Table 3.3 for a list of the permission values for the $mode, and Appendix A for information on UNIX books that explain chmod in greater depth.

 The chown command allows you to change file ownership, but only on UNIX, using user and group IDs extracted from the UNIX password file, /etc/passwd. See the online documentation for more on this command.

To truncate the data in a file, you can use the truncate command:

```
truncate($file, $new_size)
```

The $file can be either a file name or a file handle. The $new_size is usually 0, to eliminate all data in a file.

You can rename a file with the rename command:

```
$status = rename($oldname, $newname);
```

 Clever users will notice that you can use rename to move a file to a new location. But watch out, as rename won't work over file system boundaries.

To delete a file, use unlink:

```
unlink(filename);
```

To delete more than one file at once, pass a list of names to unlink:

```
unlink(filename1, filename2, filename3, ...);
```

Despite its name, unlink has nothing to do with either symbolic links or the link or symlink commands. The term unlink is historical UNIX usage and nothing more.

Symbolic Links

Most UNIX systems support links, files, or directories that really exists elsewhere but look like they exist here. You can access the file or directory in its linked location, but the real data lie elsewhere.

Symbolic links are usually used with directories, where a known location, such as **/usr/bin/X11** (where most X Window programs reside), may be linked to a different area on disk. Symbolic links oftentimes allow you to have the file system set up the way cranky software expects, but with large directories shared between systems or placed on disks with greater free space.

In Perl, the link command allows you to link an existing file or directory to a new name, often in a new location:

```
link($oldname, $newname)
```

The $oldname must exist. If the $newname exists, you'll overwrite it.

Similarly, the Perl symlink command creates a symbolic link:

```
symlink($oldname, $newname)
```

A very common mistake is to switch the $oldname, the file that exists, with the $newname, the name of the link. If you mix these up, you're likely to destroy $oldname. Watch out when using either link or symlink.

NOTE Some systems simply don't support link and symlink. Perl has been ported to just about every variety of UNIX, MS-DOS, and Windows as well as a host of other operating systems. Many of these systems provide limited—if any—support for the UNIX concepts inherent in Perl. Most UNIX systems should provide this support, but, if your system doesn't support link and symlink, Perl will generate a fatal error. To get around this fatal error, try this code snippet from the **perlfunc** online documentation:

```
$symlink_exists = (eval 'symlink("","");', $@ eq '');
```

Then, before calling symlink, verify that $symlink_exists is true.

Because a symbolic link looks like a file in one place but is really linked to a file in another place, you can use the readlink command to read the link and return the true file name that a link points to:

```
$true_file = readlink($file);
```

WARNING As you might expect, readlink is not supported on all systems.

Packages

In addition to the functions inherently supported by Perl, you can also package together a set of functions into a Perl *package*, also called a *module*.

Chapter 7 covers packages and modules in depth. For now, though, there are a few packages that can help a lot with file and directory processing. So, this next section will introduce a few packages that you'll find effective when working with files and directories.

The first—and most important—thing to know about packages is that you have to tell Perl which packages you intend to use, with the use command:

```
use packagename;
```

For example:

```
use File::Copy;
```

After the use command, you can use the subroutines within the package.

Copying Files

With the Perl commands introduced previously, you have enough ammunition to copy a file to another file. The File::Copy module simplifies this for you.

The copy function in this module takes two file names (or file handles) and copies the input file to the output file:

```
use File::Copy;


$status = copy(inputfile, outputfile);
```

The $status returned is 1 for success (true) and 0 on failure (false).

```
#
# Build up file names from
# command-line arguments.
#
# Usage:
#    copy2.pl infile outfile
#
$input = $ARGV[0];
$output = ">" . $ARGV[1];

use File::Copy;

copy($input, $output) ||
    die "Can't copy $input to $output.";

# copy2.pl
```

File::Copy is a standard Perl package, but it may not be installed on Windows.

WINDOWS

Extracting File Names from Paths

The File::Basename package provides routines to extract the directory, base name, and suffix (or extension) for a full file path. For example, you can use the fileparse function to convert a full file path, such as **/home/erc/perl/examples/copy1.pl**, into its components: */home/erc/perl/examples/*, *copy1*, and *.pl*.

To do this, call fileparse in the File::Basename package:

```
use File::Basename;

($basename,$directory_path,$suffix) =
    fileparse($fullname,@suffixlist);
```

The $fullname is the full directory path. The @suffixlist is a list of regular expressions used to match against the file name for extracting the suffix. To extract text files using a *.pl* extension, for example, set @suffixlist to the following:

```
@suffixlist = "\.pl";
```

The backslash escapes the period. You can see this in action with the following example script:

```
#
# Extracts base file name from full path.
#
use File::Basename;

  # Set up example name.
$fullname = "/usr/local/lib/perl5/validate.pl";
```

```
# Look for files ending in .pl (Perl).
@suffixlist = "\.pl";

($basename,$directory_path,$suffix) = fileparse($fullname,@suffixlist);

print "For    $fullname\n";
print "base: $basename\n";
print "path: $directory_path\n";
print "ext.: $suffix\n";

# basename.pl
```

When you run this script, with its example full path name of **/usr/local/lib/perl5/validate.pl**, you'll see the following output:

```
For    /usr/local/lib/perl5/validate.pl
base: validate
path: /usr/local/lib/perl5/
ext.: .pl
```

WINDOWS

As mentioned before (you always have to pay attention to this, alas), MS-DOS and UNIX use different directory separators. To get fileparse to work with Windows, you also need to tell File::Basename the file system type:

```
use File::Basename;

fileparse_set_fstype("MSDOS");
```

This tells fileparse to use a backslash for Windows file names. The other supported types are "VMS" and "MacOS". UNIX is the default type.

We can modify the **basename.pl** script to set the type to "MSDOS" and use a Windows-style file name, as shown next:

```
#
# Extracts base file name from full path.
```

```
# Uses Windows conventions.
#
use File::Basename;

fileparse_set_fstype("MSDOS");

   # Set up example name.
$fullname = "C:\\usr\\local\\lib\\Perl5\\validate.pl";

   # Look for files ending in .pl (Perl).
@suffixlist = "\.pl";

($basename,$directory_path,$suffix) = fileparse($fullname,@suffixlist);

print "For    $fullname\n";
print "base: $basename\n";
print "path: $directory_path\n";
print "ext.: $suffix\n";


# basename.pl
```

After running this script (on Windows or UNIX), you'll see the following results as the `fileparse_set_fstype("MSDOS");` command tells `fileparse` how to operate:

```
For    C:\usr\local\lib\Perl5\validate.pl
base: validate
path: C:\usr\local\lib\Perl5\
ext.: .pl
```

See Chapter 8 for more on detecting operating system differences.

Detecting the Current Directory

The Cwd package contains routines to return the name of the current working directory:

```
#
# Get current directory.
#

use Cwd;

$dir = getcwd;
print "Current directory is: $dir\n";


# cwd.pl
```

NOTE The Cwd package contains more than one routine to perform this task. Of the routines, the documentation claims that cwd is the safest and most portable, but it does not function properly on Hewlett-Packard systems. Hence, I used getcwd here instead.

Summary

In order to do much of anything in Perl, you need to access files and directories, and Perl provides the commands to do it. open opens a file for reading or writing (or both). read reads data from a file, while print (not write) writes data to a file. Always close a file when done.

For directories, open a directory with opendir, read it with readdir, and close it with closedir.

Perl comes with some handy packages, including File::Copy for copying files, File::Basename for parsing file names from full directory paths, and Cwd for getting the current working directory.

Perl Commands Introduced in This Chapter

binmode
chdir
chmod
close

closedir

copy (in package File::Copy)

cwd (in package Cwd)

die

eof

fileparse (in package File::Basename)

fileparse_set_fstype (in package File::Basename)

getc

getcwd (in package Cwd)

glob

link

mkdir

open

opendir

read

readdir

readlink

rename

rewinddir

rmdir

seek

stat

symlink

tell

truncate

unlink

use

CHAPTER 4

Transforming Data: Pattern Matching and Substitutions

This chapter covers:

- Searching for data in text
- Perl's regular expressions
- Substituting data
- Using tr to transform characters
- Removing leading and trailing spaces from input data

Searching for Data in Text

One of the most common tasks in Perl is combining input data for particular patterns and then processing the patterns in a particular way. This includes transforming database records into Web page data, parsing system files, and performing most other general text processing. This chapter covers how to search for and transform data.

To start, you need to find the data you want. To do this, Perl uses something called regular expressions.

Regular Expressions

Betraying its UNIX roots, Perl's regular expressions are a lot like expressions in UNIX applications such as **sed** and **vi**. Perl, however, extends this set and provides many extra features.

A *regular expression* is a construct that defines what to look for in a general way, such as any alphanumeric character, or a specific way, such as matching the text "OPEN" exactly. The way you define what to look for involves fairly complicated and obscure sequences of letters and punctuation, where all the punctuation holds special meaning.

The basic format for a regular expression is:

```
/pattern/
```

With this construct, Perl compares a text string with the pattern and returns 1 (true) or 0 (false), depending on whether there is a match. In almost all cases, you use the /pattern/ with a scalar text variable, such as the following:

```
if ($string =~ /a/) {

   # If an 'a' was found...
}
```

The preceding code compares the value in $string with the pattern /a/. If there is a match, the expression resolves to true; if there is no match, the expression resolves to false. If you omit the variable, then the value in $_, the hidden default variable, gets compared to the pattern:

```
# Compare against value in $_
if (/a/) {

   # If an 'a' was found...
}
```

You can also compare in reverse, that is, check if the pattern doesn't match, using the following syntax:

```
if ($string !~ /a/) {

    # If no 'a' was found...
}
```

You can build up complicated regular expressions using the patterns in Table 4.1.

Table 4.1 Regular expression patterns.

Pattern	Interpretation
/a/	Looks for any instance of *a*.
/a+/	Matches one or more instances of *a*.
/a*/	Matches zero or more instances of *a*.
/a?/	Matches zero or one instance of *a*.
/a|b/	Matches either *a* or *b*.

Most of Perl's regular expression syntax comes from the UNIX program **egrep**.

U N I X

You can also place variables inside patterns. In that case, /$a/ means to match against the value of $a, which is placed in the pattern when the pattern is compiled.

You can use square brackets, [and], to delimit a range of characters. [aA], for example, means either *a* or *A*. [a-z] matches any lowercase character, while [0-9] matches any digit. You can combine the brackets with other patterns, as shown in Table 4.2.

Table 4.2 Adding brackets to regular expressions.

Pattern	Interpretation
/[aA]/	Matches against *a* or *A*.
/[aA]+/	Matches one or more instances of *a* or *A*.
/[aA]*/	Matches zero or more instances of *a* or *A*.
/[aA]?/	Matches zero or one instance of *a* or *A*.
/[^aA]/	Returns true if any character is found that is not *a* or *A*.
/[aB]|[bB]/	Matches an instance of *a* or *A* or *b* or *B*; redundant in this case, as it is the same as /[aAbB]/.

With the square bracket ranges, there are a number of commonly used patterns, such as [0-9] for any digit and [_0-9a-zA-Z] for characters allowed in variable names. To save typing, Perl provides shortcuts for these common patterns; They are listed in Table 4.3.

Table 4.3 Looking in only specified locations.

Pattern	Interpretation
/\d/	Any digit.
/\D/	Anything other than a digit.
/\w/	Any word character, i.e., [_0-9a-zA-Z].
/\W/	Anything other than a word character.
/s	Any white space (tab, return, space, or newline).
/\S/	Anything other than white space.
/./	Any character except a newline.

The \w pattern matches a single character, not a whole word. To match against a word, try \w+.

The concept of *white space* comes from UNIX, where it is defined as any blank space in a document. In Perl terms, a white space character is a space, tab, carriage return, form feed, or newline.

N O T E

You can make very complex patterns by combining the simpler forms. For example, to match a pattern that begins with an *a*, has a number of characters, and ends with an *a*, you can use /a.*a/. Broken down to its elements, this is a, then any number of any characters except a newline, .*, then a. The * allows for zero or more matches of the preceding element, so the .* pattern matches any number of any characters, except a newline.

Greedy Searches: Perl's regular expressions are said to be *greedy*. That means each pattern will try to match as much as it can. Thus, the pattern /a.*a/ matches as many characters as possible between the *as*. So, if your text string is *anaconda*, /a.*a/ will match the whole string, because it has an *a* followed by many characters until the final *a*. This pattern will not match the *ana* part of *anaconda* due to the greedy rule: match as much as possible that follows the pattern.

You can search for a pattern at a specified location, such as the beginning or end of the string, as shown in Table 4.4.

Table 4.4 Searching in only specified locations.

Pattern	Interpretation
/^a/	Match against *a* only at beginning of string.
/a$/	Match against *a* only at end of string.
/a\b/	Match *a* at end of word.
/a\B/	Match *a* not at end of word.

Perl uses a dollar sign, $, to signify a scalar variable, and this tends to be confused with the /a$/ pattern. /$a/ means to match the value of $a, while /a$/ matches against an a at the end of the string. To further complicate it, /a/ matches against the value of *a* at the end of the string.

The ^ character acts differently when it is inside a square bracket from when it is not. This means /^a/ and /[^a]/ are very different. /^a/ looks for *a* at the start of the string. /[^a]/ will return true if there is any character not *a* anywhere in the word.

Table 4.5 shows how you can control how many occurrences of a pattern you're looking for.

Table 4.5 Multiple occurrences in the pattern.

Pattern	Interpretation
/a{1,4}/	Matches 1, 2, 3, or 4 *a*s.
/a{2}/	Matches 2 *a*s.
/a{0,2}/	Matches 1 or 2 *a*s.

That's a lot of variation. You can use these relatively simple constructs to create increasingly complex patterns. For example, in most programming or scripting languages, a variable name must begin with a letter and can be followed by any number of letters, digits, or underscore (_) characters. You can use the following pattern to match this:

```
/^[a-zA-Z]+[_0-9a-zA-Z]*$/
```

This pattern ensures that the beginning of the string has one or more alphabetical characters and is followed, to the end of the string, by zero or more digits, alphabetical characters, or underscores. The ^ and $ are essential to make this pattern work or patterns like 2ab3 would match against the pattern. The match actually occurs starting at ab3. The ^ and $ ensure that the whole word (the whole string) is checked.

N O T E Variable names in Perl aren't limited by these arbitrary rules. This is just a common test.

These patterns get exceedingly complex. To help manage the complexity, you can use parentheses to control the order in which the pattern is evaluated.

Changing the Delimiter

On UNIX systems, you often need to search for patterns within data that contain forward slashes, such as searching for a pattern within a file name.

Using the m command, you can specify a different delimiter. The m command works exactly like the patterns, only you specify the delimiter. For example, to use | as a delimiter when matching a file name, you can use the following pattern:

```
m|^/usr/local/|
```

This pattern matches against /usr/local/ in the beginning of the string.

To help make sense of Perl patterns, the following **pattern.pl** script tests many of the combinations:

```
#
# Patternmatching in Perl.
#
# Usage:
#   Perl pattern.pl patt
#
# Where patt is the pattern you
# want to test.
#
foreach $patt (@ARGV) {

    print "Checking \"$patt\"\n";

    # Check for a.
    if ($patt =~ /a/) {
        print "\tFound an a:\"$patt\".\n";
    }

    # Check for no a.
    if ($patt !~ /a/) {
        print "\tNO a:\"$patt\".\n";
    }

    # Check for a or b.
    if ($patt =~ /a|b/) {
        print "\tFound an a or b:\"$patt\".\n";
    }
```

```perl
# Check for digit.
if ($patt =~ /\d/) {
    print "\tFound a digit:\"$patt\".\n";
}

# Check for no digit.
if ($patt =~ /\D/) {
    print "\tFound non-digit: \"$patt\".\n";
}

# Check for white space.
if ($patt =~ /\s/) {
    print "\tFound white space:\"$patt\".\n";
}

# Check beginning.
if ($patt =~ /^perl/) {
    print "\tFound perl at start: \"$patt\".\n";
}

# Check end.
if ($patt =~ /perl$/) {
    print "\tFound perl at end: \"$patt\".\n";
}

# Check beginning and end.
if ($patt =~ /^perl$/) {
    print "\tFound only perl: \"$patt\".\n";
}

# Include a variable inside the patt.
$a = "perl";

if ($patt =~ /$a$/) {
    print "\tFound $a at end of \"$patt\".\n";
}

# Check for 4-8 a's.
```

```
    if ($patt =~ /a{4,8}/) {
        print "\tFound 4-8 a's:\"$patt\".\n";
    }
```

```
    # Check for leading alpha character,
    # rest alphanumeric.
    if ($patt =~ /^[a-zA-Z]+[_0-9a-zA-Z]*$/) {
        print "\tLeading alpha, alphanumeric:\"$patt\".\n";
    }

    # Use a different delimiter.
    if ($patt =~ m|/usr/local/|) {
        print "\tFound /usr/local/:\"$patt\".\n";
    }

}

# pattern.pl
```

When you run this script, you pass it a number of patterns on the command line.

NOTE

To pass a pattern with spaces, use double quotes on the command line, such as "a b".

To test this script and verify that search patterns work the way you think, try the following command:

```
perl pattern.pl perl /usr/local/bin/ "a b" 1ab3
```

You should see output like the following:

```
Checking "perl"
        NO a:"perl".
        Found non-digit: "perl".
        Found perl at start: "perl".
        Found perl at end: "perl".
```

```
        Found only perl: "perl".
        Found perl at end of "perl".
        Leading alpha, alphanumeric:"perl".
Checking "/usr/local/bin/"
        Found an a:"/usr/local/bin/".
        Found an a or b:"/usr/local/bin/".
        Found non-digit: "/usr/local/bin/".
        Found /usr/local/:"/usr/local/bin/".
Checking "a b"
        Found an a:"a b".
        Found an a or b:"a b".
        Found non-digit: "a b".
        Found white space:"a b".
Checking "1ab3"
        Found an a:"1ab3".
        Found an a or b:"1ab3".
        Found a digit:"1ab3".
        Found non-digit: "1ab3".
```

Pattern-Matching Options

You can add options to the end of a pattern, after the final /, using the letters in Table 4.6.

Table 4.6 Search pattern options.

Option	Usage
/*pattern*/g	Match globally, i.e., find all occurrences.
/*pattern*/i	Do case-insensitive pattern matching.
/*pattern*/m	Treat string as multiple lines.
/*pattern*/o	Only compile pattern once; used with variables in patterns.
/*pattern*/s	Treat string as single line.

You can use the g option and regular expressions to extract data into list elements. Look in the online Perl documentation on Perl operators (**perlop**) for more on these options and the more complex patterns.

Up to now, all the patterns were used to query whether the input data match the pattern. You can also use Perl's patterns to substitute data.

Using Patterns with Substitutions

The s operator substitutes data that matches a pattern with replacement data. The patterns follow the guidelines listed earlier. To use the s operator, use the following syntax:

```
$variable =~ s/pattern/substitution/;
```

The s operator returns the number of substitutions made or 0 if none occurred. For example, if I receive a large promotion and want to change my Web home page, I could use the following substitution:

```
#
# Substituting job titles.
#
$p = "Eric Johnson, Software Engineer";

$p =~ s/Software Engineer/Grand High Pooh Bah/;

print "New title: $p.\n";

# position.pl
```

Now, if only I could get my employer to agree.

One common use for substitutions is to clean up input data. For example, you may need to clear out all leading and trailing white space from data in a file before you can process the data. To do this, you can use the following script as a guide:

```
#
# Strips leading and trailing
# white space from all lines in
# input files and prints the
# transformed lines to STDOUT.
#
# Usage:
#   perl stripsp.pl file name file name ...
#
foreach $i (0 .. $#ARGV) {

     open(INPUT, $ARGV[$i])
          || die "Can't open $ARGV[$i].";

     # Read each line into $_.
     while (<INPUT>) {

          # Put read-in line into string.
          $string = $_;

          # Remove trailing white space.
          &remove_trailing($string);

          # Remove leading white space.
          &remove_leading($string);

          # Print string to STDOUT.
          print "$string\n";
     }

     close(INPUT);
}

#
# Subroutine to strip leading white space
# from a string.
```

```
#
# Usage:
#    &remove_leading($string);
#
sub remove_leading {
    local($string) = $_[0];

    $string =~ s/^\s*//;

    # Place output in original string.
    $_[0] = $string;
}


#
# Subroutine removes trailing white space
# from a string.
#
# Usage:
#    &remove_trailing($string);
#
sub remove_trailing {
    local($string) = $_[0];

    $string =~ s/\s*$//;

    # Place output in original string.
    $_[0] = $string;
}

# stripsp.pl
```

The **stripsp.pl** script reads in files and prints out each line with all leading and trailing white space removed. Chances are you won't want to just print out such data, you'll want to use the remove_leading and remove_trailing subroutines to help preprocess your data and make it easier to parse.

Controlling the Delimiter

With substitutions, you can specify a delimiter other than / by placing the new delimiter character right after the s. For example, to convert a UNIX file path of **/usr/bin** to **/usr/local/bin**, which makes extensive use of the / character, you can use the following substitution:

```
#
# Changing substitution delimiters.
#
$path = "/usr/bin";

$path =~ s|/usr/bin|/usr/local/bin|;

print "New path: $path.\n";

# path.pl
```

Extracting Data with Substitutions

The s operator supports a number of variables, including $&, which contain the matched string, $` (a back-tick character), which contains everything before the matched string; and $', which contains everything after the matched string.

The s operator also supports a number of options, as shown in Table 4.7.

Table 4.7 Options for the s operator.

Option	Meaning
s/*pattern*/*substitution*/g	Replace all matches of pattern (global).
s/*pattern*/*substitution*/i	Ignore case in matching.
s/*pattern*/*substitution*/e	Evaluate substitution as an expression.
s/*pattern*/*substitution*/o	Compile expression only once (for variable values, etc.).
s/*pattern*/*substitution*/m	Treat string as multiple lines.
s/*pattern*/*substitution*/s	Treat string as a single line.

See the online documentation on Perl operators (**perlop**) for more information on these options and on substitution in general.

Transforming Data with tr

Similar to the pattern matching described so far, the tr command transforms text data, usually replacing one type of character with another.

The syntax for the tr command looks like the following:

```
tr/search/substitution/;
```

Unlike the s operator, however, tr substitutes data on a character-by-character basis, transforming each search character with the corresponding substitution character. The following command does not search for a pattern of *abc*:

```
tr/abc/123/;
```

Instead, it replaces each occurrence of *a* with *1*, *b* with *2*, and *c* with *3*. Obviously, this is not the same as with the s operator.

Like the preceding command, if you omit a =~ or !~ operator, then tr modifies the value held in $_, the default variable for most commands. In normal usage, you'll use the =~ operator to transform a scalar value, such as the following:

```
$newname =~ tr/A-Z/a-z/;
```

tr does not support all the regular expression pattern characters, such as *, + and ?, because it looks for individual characters to replace with other characters. tr returns the number of characters it transformed.

There are a number of obscure options you can place after the tr command to modify the way tr works, as shown in Table 4.8.

Table 4.8 tr options.

Option	Usage
tr/*search*/*substitution*/c	Complement the search, i.e., replace everything not in the search pattern.
tr/*search*/*substitution*/d	Delete all characters found that are not replaced.
tr/*search*/*substitution*/s	Squash duplicate replaced characters.

With the /s squash option, multiple spaces, for example, get converted to a single space. See the online Perl reference material for more on these options.

NOTE

If you're familiar with **sed**, the tr command acts like the **sed** y command. In Perl, you can use y in place of tr; both perform the same function.

Using tr to Convert File Names

A very handy use of tr is to convert all lowercase file names to uppercase, or vice versa. If you network UNIX and PC systems, you'll often find that when copying files back and forth, file names tend to get mapped to all uppercase or all lowercase, depending on the program used for copying. Sometimes, you need to go in and clean up the file names, changing them to all upper- or all lowercase letters.

For this, tr is perfect. We can put together a very simple script that converts all the file names passed on the command line into upper- or lowercase.

These two tasks are virtually the same. Starting with a conversion to lowercase, we can use the following script:

```
#
# Convert all file names passed in to
# lowercase.
#
```

```
foreach $filename (@ARGV) {

    $newname = $filename;

    # Convert uppercase to lower.
    $newname =~ tr/[A-Z]/[a-z]/;

    #
    # Only rename if different and
    # the $newname doesn't already exist.
    #
    if ($newname ne $filename) {

        #
        # If the new name already exists,
        # don't clobber this file.
        #
        if ( -e $newname ) {

            print "ERROR: Won't clobber existing $newname.\n";

        } else {

            print "Renaming $filename to $newname.\n";
            rename($filename, $newname);
        }
    }

}

# tolower.pl
```

This script goes through each command-line argument, assuming that each names a file. The `tr` command converts the name to lowercase:

```
$newname =~ tr/[A-Z]/[a-z]/;
```

The script then calls the rename function (see the Chapter 3) to rename the old $filename to the $newname. There's a problem if you already have a file with the new name: rename will destroy the existing file. To avoid this, you should check whether a file already exists with the new name:

```
if ( -e $newname ) {

    # Print an error message.
}
```

The Windows FAT file system is not case-sensitive when it comes to reading a file. Thus, the preceding test will likely fail if you use a FAT file system.

WINDOWS

Another potential problem is if the file name is already all lowercase. That's why the **tolower.pl** script verifies that the new name and the old name don't match:

```
if ($newname ne $filename) {

    # Names don't match, so OK to rename.
}
```

For example, to convert the file names **A** and **B** to lowercase, you can use the following command:

```
perl tolower.pl A B
```

This will generate the following output (presuming you have files named **A** and **B**):

```
Renaming A to a.
Renaming B to b.
```

If you already have a file named **a** in your current directory, this script will generate an error message like the following:

```
ERROR: Won't clobber existing a.
```

To convert all file names to uppercase, you only need to change the `tr` command; the rest of the script remains the same, as shown in the **toupper.pl** script:

```perl
#
# Convert all file names passed in to
# uppercase.
#
foreach $filename (@ARGV) {

    $newname = $filename;

    # Convert lowercase to upper.
    $newname =~ tr/[a-z]/[A-Z]/;

    #
    # Only rename if different and
    # the $newname doesn't already exist.
    #
    if ($newname ne $filename) {

        #
        # If the new name already exists,
        # don't clobber this file.
        #
        if ( -e $newname ) {

            print "ERROR: Won't clobber existing $newname.\n";

        } else {
```

```
        print "Renaming $filename to $newname.\n";
        rename($filename, $newname);
    }
  }
}

# toupper.pl
```

Summary

Perl's regular expressions provide you with a powerful means for searching for particular elements within textual data. A regular expression is a construct that defines what to look for. The basic format for a regular expression is /pattern/.

The m command allows you to change the default delimiter, /, to some other character.

The s command uses regular expressions to substitute data that matches a pattern.

The simpler tr command transforms characters, such as converting characters from uppercase to lowercase.

Perl Commands Introduced in This Chapter

m

s

tr

y

## CHAPTER 5

Formatting Reports

This chapter covers:

- Report formats
- Page headers
- Controlling pagination
- The `printf` and `sprintf` functions
- Getting the time and date
- Databases and Perl
- DBM databases

Reports

Back in the days before most offices had laser printers, formatting reports to fixed-size character widths was not only important but also an art form. Now, with more modern equipment, such reports rarely use a line of dashes or equal signs to mark out separators. Even so, you'll find Perl a powerful engine for outputting formatted data. In this chapter, you'll learn about Perl formats and how `write` is not the opposite of `read`.

With this chapter, we get into the meat of Perl, which was originally designed to aid in creating system status reports for UNIX system administrators. The part that doesn't always work well is that with modern laser printers and Web pages, you're rarely using a fixed-width font as Perl assumes.

The whole idea of reporting starts with the concept that you have data, most likely lots of data. Chances are that the data aren't in a format that's immediately useful. So, you want to print out (to a file or to paper) a set of data formatted in such a way that you can actually use the information.

In Perl, the way you start is to define a format.

Formats

A *format* defines how data written to a file will appear. The format defines where the data will go and how many digits will be used. In addition, the format defines the surrounding text that, you hope, will make the report more understandable.

The `format` command defines a format:

```
format NAME =
formatdata

.
```

The `format` ends with a single period on a line, something that's easy to forget.

The format data come in pairs of lines. In each pair, the first line lists how the data will look; the second line lists the global Perl variables that will hold the data.

For example,

```
format NAMES=
Last name:  @<<<<<<<<<<<<<<<<<<<<<<
$lastname
First name: @<<<<<<<<<<<<
$firstname


.
```

The preceding format, called `NAMES`, displays two data fields, with data from variables `$lastname` and `$firstname`. The funny-looking

@<<<<<<<<<<< defines a left-justified data field. The number of < characters defines how many spaces are allotted for the field. The lines with variables, $lastname and $firstname, aren't printed. Just the lines that define the format are printed. See the output of the **format1.pl** script for more on this.

Formats in Perl assume that your output will use a fixed-width font.

N O T E

Using Formats

The format command defines how a report will look. Normally, the format defines how each individual record will look, but additional enhancements are covered later.

Once you've defined a format, output the data with the write command. The write command acts a lot like the PRINT USING command in BASIC. The write command takes one argument, the file handle where the data should get written:

```
write filehandle;
```

You can make the *filehandle* optional if you use the Perl select function to make a particular file handle the default file handle for write's output. See the section entitled "Selecting File Handles," for more information.

N O T E

To use write with a format, name the format the same name as you use for the Perl file handle when you open the file for output. Then, after opening the file, repeat the following process:

1. Fill in the variables ($lastname and $firstname in this case) with data from one record.
2. Call the write command.

Repeat this process for each record of data. For example, the following code uses the simple format already shown:

```
#
# Example of Perl's formats.
# Usage:
#    Perl format1.pl reportfile

# Set up format.
format NAMES=
Last name:  @<<<<<<<<<<<<<<<<<<<<<<
$lastname
First name: @<<<<<<<<<<<
$firstname


.

# Open file.
open(NAMES, ">$ARGV[0]" )
 or die "Can't open $ARGV[0]";

# Output first record.
$lastname  = "Cleveland";
$firstname = "Grover";

write NAMES;

# Output next record.
$lastname  = "Fillmore";
$firstname = "Millard";

write NAMES;

# Close file.
close(NAMES);

# format1.pl
```

When you run the script, it will output the following data to the file name you provide on the command line:

```
Last name:  Cleveland
First name: Grover

Last name:  Fillmore
First name: Millard
```

Each call to write outputs three lines: the last name, the first name and a blank line to separate the records. Note how the blank lines between the records matches the blank line in the format.

For most usage, that's all you need to know about reports in Perl. Of course, there are some more options.

Defining Formats

The @<<<<<<<<<<<< in the preceding format defines a left-justified field. You can also define right-justified or centered fields using the syntax shown in Table 5.1.

Table 5.1 Format field types.

Format	Meaning
@<<<<<	Left-justified field.
@>>>>>	Right-justified field.
@|||||	Centered field.
@#####.##	Numeric field with given decimal digits, right justified.

In each case, the number of special characters defines the number of spaces allotted for the field in the report.

Perl also supports multiline fields. See the online documentation on **perl-form** for more information.

N O T E

If you have multiple data fields on the same line, separate the variables with commas, as shown here:

```
format WORKORDER=
Ship: @<<<<<<<<<<<<<<<<<<<     Priority: @>>>>>>>
$ship, $priority
Description: @<<<<<<<<<<<<<<<<<<<<<<<<<<<<<<<<<
$description
Access:      @<<<<<<<<<<<<<<<<<<<<<<<<<<<<<<<<<
$access
Deck: @<<    Stardate: @########.#
$deck, $stardate
.
```

We can use this format in a sample work-order application for Star Trek engineers, as shown next:

```
#
# Example of Perl's formats.
# Usage:
#    Perl format2.pl reportfile

# Set up format.
format WORKORDER=
Ship: @<<<<<<<<<<<<<<<<<<<     Priority: @>>>>>>>
$ship, $priority
Description: @<<<<<<<<<<<<<<<<<<<<<<<<<<<<<<<<<
$description
Access:      @<<<<<<<<<<<<<<<<<<<<<<<<<<<<<<<<<
$access
Deck: @<<    Stardate: @########.#
$deck, $stardate
.

# Open file.
open(WORKORDER, ">$ARGV[0]" )
```

```
  or die "Can't open $ARGV[0]";

# Output record.

$description = "Reconfigure phase inducer";
$ship        = "Voyager";
$priority     = "Urgent";
$access       = "Via Jefferies Tube";
$deck         = 17;
$stardate     = 95201.4;

write WORKORDER;

# Output record.

$description = "Recalibrate sensor array";
$ship        = "Voyager";
$priority     = "Urgent";
$access       = "Via Jefferies Tube";
$deck         = 12;
$stardate     = 95203.5;

write WORKORDER;

# Output record.

$description = "Remodulate tachyon beam emitter";
$ship        = "Voyager";
$priority     = "Urgent";
$access       = "Via Jefferies Tube";
$deck         = 10;
$stardate     = 95212.0;

write WORKORDER;

# Close file.
close(WORKORDER);

# format2.pl
```

When you run this script, the output data will look like the following:

```
Ship: Voyager                    Priority:      Urgent
Description: Reconfigure phase inducer
Access:         Via Jefferies Tube
Deck: 17       Stardate:      95201.4


Ship: Voyager                    Priority:      Urgent
Description: Recalibrate sensor array
Access:         Via Jefferies Tube
Deck: 12       Stardate:      95203.5


Ship: Voyager                    Priority:      Urgent
Description: Remodulate tachyon beam emitter
Access:         Via Jefferies Tube
Deck: 10       Stardate:      95212.0
```

Most reports appear with fancy headers at the top of each page. The page header may list the page number, column headings, and so on. In Perl, you can define a special format to print at the top of each page.

Page Headers

The name of the page header format must be the same as the name of your file handle, with a _TOP appended to the file handle name. For example, the following is a page header format for the WORKORDER file handle:

```
format WORKORDER_TOP=
Starfleet Work Orders

.
```

One of the most common elements you'll want to put into your formats is the page number. Perl stores this in the $% variable.

To add the page number to your top-of-page format, treat $% like any other variable and add it to the format, as shown here:

```
# Top-of-page format, displays page number.
```

```
format WORKORDER_TOP=
Starfleet Work Orders, page @<<<
$%
```

.

You can place as much data as you'd like in the top-of-page format, but if you use too many lines, there won't be any room left for the report.

Once you set up such a format, it will print at the top of each output page.

Perl doesn't yet support page footers, data that are printed at the bottom of each page.

NOTE

Controlling Pagination

Perl also provides some control over pagination through the use of special variables.

The `$=` variable holds the number of lines allowed on a page. When the line number exceeds this amount, `write` outputs a new page. `$=` defaults to 60, which may or may not be appropriate for your printer.

The `$-` variable counts down as each line gets output on a page. When `$-` gets to 0, `write` outputs a new page. You can take advantage of this and set `$-` to 0 to force a page output on the next call to `write`.

According to the Perl documentation, setting `$-` to 0 is all you need to do. The next `write` should advance to the next page. The problem is that this doesn't work. Setting `$-` works only if you have a top-of-page format, e.g., `FILEHANDLE_TOP`. If you set up the top-of-page format, you can then set `$-` to 0 to force a page output on the next `write`.

WARNING

Don't mix calls to `print` and `write` with the same file handle. When you use `write`, the `$-` variable gets automatically updated, but when you use `print`, it doesn't. Also, `write` may lose its place in the output file if you mix the `print` and `write` functions, so don't do it.

WARNING

When `write` outputs a new page, it prints the data in the `$^L` variable, which presumably advances the page. `$^L` defaults to the formfeed character, which is often represented in UNIX as `^L` (hence `$^L`).

Selecting File Handles

A separate version of each of the pagination variables exists for each file handle. The way you tell them apart is with the `select` function.

The `select` function marks a file handle as the default handle. Without specifying a file handle, any `print` or `write` statement will output to the currently selected file. When Perl starts up, the default file handle selected is `STDOUT`.

So, if you want to modify the `$-`, `$=`, or any other print-specific variable, you first need to call `select` on the desired file handle. To select a file handle, use the following syntax:

```
select(FILEHANDLE);
```

This `select` makes a file handle the default handle. It has nothing to do with TCP/IP network sockets nor the C `select()` function call.

Table 5.2 lists the variables relating to pages and formats.

Table 5.2 Pagination variables.

Variable	Usage
$=	Number of lines on a page; defaults to 60.
$-	Number of lines left on the page.
$%	Current page number.
$~	Name of format, defaults to same names a file handle.
$^	Name of top-of-page format, defaults to _TOP added to file handle.
$^L	String to output to advance page, defaults to formfeed character.

To test the ability to force a page to output, we need to do three things. First, set up a top-of-page format to allow pagination to work properly. Second, call `select` on the file handle. Third, set `$-` to 0 so that the next call to `write` will output a new page.

To test all this, you can modify the preceding **format2.pl** script and force each Star Trek work order to appear on its own page, as shown in **format3.pl**:

```
#
# Example of Perl's formats,
# with _TOP top of page format.
#
# Usage:
#    perl format3.pl reportfile

# Set up format.
format WORKORDER=
Ship: @<<<<<<<<<<<<<<<<<<<<    Priority: @>>>>>>>
$ship, $priority
Description: @<<<<<<<<<<<<<<<<<<<<<<<<<<<<<<<<<<<
$description
Access:      @<<<<<<<<<<<<<<<<<<<<<<<<<<<<<<<<<<<
$access
Deck: @<<    Stardate: @########.#
$deck, $stardate

.


# Top-of-page format, displays page number.
format WORKORDER_TOP=
Starfleet Work Orders, page @<<<
$%

.


# Open file.
open(WORKORDER, ">$ARGV[0]" )
 or die "Can't open $ARGV[0]";
```

```
# Make file handle default.
select(WORKORDER);

$description = "Reconfigure phase inducer";
$ship        = "Voyager";
$priority     = "Urgent";
$access       = "Via Jefferies Tube";
$deck         = 17;
$stardate     = 95201.4;

write WORKORDER;

# Output page.
$- = 0;

$description = "Recalibrate sensor array";
$ship        = "Voyager";
$priority     = "Urgent";
$access       = "Via Jefferies Tube";
$deck         = 12;
$stardate     = 95203.5;

write WORKORDER;

# Output page.
$- = 0;

$description = "Remodulate tachyon beam emitter";
$ship        = "Voyager";
$priority     = "Urgent";
$access       = "Via Jefferies Tube";
$deck         = 10;
$stardate     = 95212.0;

write WORKORDER;

# Close file.
close(WORKORDER);

# format3.pl
```

Once you select a file handle, you can set $~ to the name of any format. This frees you from having to name your formats the same as you name the file handles. You can also set $^ to the name of the format for handling the top-of-page condition.

N O T E

135

Other Means to Control Data Output

In addition to `print` and `write`, two other commands allow you to format data for output—`printf` and `sprintf`. `sprintf` returns a formatted string, and `printf` formats a string and prints it to the given file handle:

```
sprintf (format_string, data...);
printf FILEHANDLE (format_string, data...);
```

Like `print`, if you omit the file handle, `printf` outputs to the default—currently selected—file handle.

Yes, these functions act nearly the same as the C `sprintf()` and `printf()`.

C

The way both `sprintf` and `printf` work is to look at the format strings and to insert data into them. The data are assumed to appear, in order, in the remaining part of the parameters to `sprintf` or `printf`. The data are then inserted into the format string, generating the full output.

For example, the `%s` format string specifies to insert a string in place of `%s`. This string must appear after the format string as a parameter to `sprintf` or `printf`.

If you create a badly formed format string, or omit necessary parameters, `sprintf` and `printf` may cause your script—and the Perl interpreter—to crash.

WARNING

To print a single text string using %s, you can use the following command:

```
printf("%s\n", "This is a string");
```

This will print

```
This is a string
```

In this simple example, there's no real reason not to use the simpler print function, which is shown next:

```
print "This is a string\n";
```

But printf (and sprintf) provide a lot more. You can insert multiple values:

```
printf("%s's %s is named %s.\n",
    "Eric", "cat", "Halloween");
```

With the preceding command, you'll see

```
Eric's cat is named Halloween.
```

You can also insert other values, including integers, floating-point numbers with decimal control, and individual characters. Table 5.3 lists the more common printf and sprintf format options (see the online documentation for more).

Table 5.3 Format options for sprintf and printf.

Option	Meaning
%c	Insert a single character.
%d	Insert an integer value.
%e	Insert a floating-point value in scientific notation format.
%f	Insert a floating-point value.

%g	Insert a floating-point value in scientific notation format.
%i	Insert a signed integer value.
%o	Insert an integer in octal (base 8) format.
%s	Insert a string value.
%u	Insert an unsigned integer value.
%x	Insert an integer and display in hexadecimal (base 16) format. (%X forces the hexadecimal digits to appear uppercase.)

You can also control the number of characters used to format the strings. For example, %3d specifies that the integer number should be displayed with three digits. The format string of %.2f specifies a floating-point number with two decimal digits.

The example script **printf.pl** shows many of these options:

```
#
# Using printf.
#

# Strings.
printf("%s\n", "This is a string");

printf("%s's %s is named %s.\n",
    "Eric", "cat", "Halloween");

# Integers.
$x = 123;
$y = 1234;
$z = 1;

printf("Notice how z is expanded.\n");
printf("\t x=%3d y=%4d z=%5d\n", $x, $y, $z);

# Floating-point.
$f = 123.45;
```

```
printf("f=%.2f, f=%.5f, f=%3.2f, f=%1.2f\n", $f, $f, $f, $f);

# Hexadecimal.
$wid = 255;

printf("Window ID=%x\n", $wid);

# printf.pl
```

When you run the **printf.pl** script, you'll see the following output:

```
This is a string
Eric's cat is named Halloween.
Notice how z is expanded.
        x=123 y=1234 z=    1
f=123.45, f=123.45000, f=123.45, f=123.45
Window ID=ff
```

The `sprintf` function acts in much the same way as `printf`. `printf` prints its data, while `sprintf` returns the string it formats, which you can then place in a variable. This means that `printf` is really the same as:

```
print FILEHANDLE sprintf(format_string, data...);
```

The script below shows `sprintf` in operation:

```
#
# Using sprintf.
#

$str = sprintf("%s's %s is named %s.\n",
    "Eric", "cat", "Halloween");

print "$str";

# sprintf.pl
```

Putting the Date into Your Reports

Perl provides a number of functions for getting the current date and time. These functions follow the C language conventions.

The time function returns a large integer value based on the number of seconds from the start of some epoch. (On UNIX, the epoch started on 1 January, 1970. On Windows, the start of the epoch is 1 January, 1980. This means that you normally don't want to use the values returned by time directly.)

The value returned be time isn't very useful in and of itself. To extract some useful information from the time value, call gmtime for Greenwich mean time or localtime for the local time. Most people (unless you live in the Greenwich time zone) use local time. The local time should also take into account factors such as daylight savings time. (Since all this is based on your system clock, having your system set to the proper time helps.)

In Perl, localtime converts a time value into an array of nine elements:

```
($sec,$min,$hour,$dom,$mon,
 $year,$wday,$yday,$isdst) =
    localtime($time);
```

The gmtime acts similarly but returns Greenwich time:

```
($sec,$min,$hour,$dom,$mon,
 $year,$wday,$yday,$isdst) =
    gmtime($time);
```

Table 5.4 lists the values returned by both functions.

Table 5.4 Array values returned by localtime and gmtime functions.

Value	Holds
$sec	Seconds after the minute, from 0 to 59.
$min	Minutes after the hour, from 0 to 59.

`$hour`	Hour of day, from 0 to 23.
`$dom`	Day of month, from 1 to 31.
`$mon`	Month of year, from 0 to 11.
`$year`	Years since 1900.
`$wday`	Days since Sunday, from 0 to 6.
`$yday`	Days since January 1, from 0 to 365.
`$isdst`	Daylight savings time; > 0 if in effect, 0 if not, < 0 if Perl can't tell.

Note that many of the values start counting at zero, so you may need to adjust the values before printing. Alternatively, you can use the value to index into a Perl array and print out a more common name of the month, day of the week, and so on.

For example,

```
@months = ("January", "February",
          "March", "April", "May",
          "June", "July", "August",
          "September", "October",
          "November", "December");

@week = ("Sunday", "Monday", "Tuesday",
         "Wednesday", "Thursday",
         "Friday", "Saturday");

$year += 1900;

printf("Date is: %s, %d-%s-%d\n",
       $week[$wday], $dom, $months[$mon],
       $year);
```

To extract the current date, then, you can use the following Perl script:

```
#
# Using time and localtime.
#
$t = time();
```

```
($sec, $min, $hour, $dom, $mon,
 $year,$wday, $yday, $isdst) =
   localtime($t);

# Convert data to normal values.
$hour++;   # from 0..23

$year += 1900;

# Provide English equivalents.
@months = ("January", "February",
           "March", "April", "May",
           "June", "July", "August",
           "September", "October",
           "November", "December");

@week = ("Sunday", "Monday", "Tuesday",
         "Wednesday", "Thursday",
         "Friday", "Saturday");

# Print data.

printf ("Time is: %2.2d:%2.2d:%2.2d\n",
    $hour, $min, $sec);

printf("Date is: %s, %d-%s-%d\n",
    $week[$wday], $dom, $months[$mon],
    $year);

printf("%d days since 1 January\n",
    $yday);

if ($isdst) {
    print "Is daylight savings time.\n";
} else {
    print "No daylight savings time.\n";
}

# time1.pl
```

When you run this script, you'll see output like the following (presuming you live in the past):

```
Time is: 10:56:03
Date is: Friday, 3-May-1996
123 days since 1 January
Is daylight savings time.
```

If instead of an array, you set the value of localtime to a scalar variable, you'll get a typical UNIX-style time, as shown here:

```
#
# Placing time in a scalar,
# rather than an array.
#
$t = time();

$now = localtime($t);

print "Time is: $now\n";

# time2.pl
```

The output of this script looks like the following:

```
Time is: Fri May  3 10:56:03 1996
```

So, armed with the time and localtime functions, you can then place the current date and time into your reports by setting the data into variables used in your formats.

Databases and Perl

Perl's reports are most useful when you have data to report. And, one of the largest sources of data to generate reports comes from databases.

Perl's strong text-handling capabilities make Perl ideal for extracting data from databases, formatting the data, and then displaying reports using the `write` command.

Special Perl modules, which appear later in this chapter, provide interfaces to popular database systems such as Oracle and Sybase. In addition, Perl provides routines to interface with UNIX DBM databases.

DBM Databases

Most UNIX systems provide a simple database system called DBM, short for data base management. DBM is also often called ndbm for new DBM, or gdbm for GNU DBM. DBM databases manage data that are stored in key/value pairs. You can access any value by its key. Look familiar? This looks suspiciously close to Perl's associative arrays.

The current version of Perl for Win32 doesn't support the `dbmopen` and `dbmclose` functions. These functions will not error. Data will simply not get written to a DBM database. Your best bet on Windows is to connect Perl to a database, such as Borland dBASE. Perl is especially good at handling things like ASCII-delimited dBASE files.

WINDOWS

While not intended for heavyweight usage, you can use DBM databases to make Perl associative arrays persistent. That is, you can use DBM to store the data to disk so that the array can be read in during another run of the program or from any other program.

`dbmopen` associates a DBM database, which includes two files with a Perl associative array—a data file and an index file. `dbmopen` takes the following syntax:

```
dbmopen(%assoc, $database, $mode) or
   die "Can't open \"$database\"";
```

The `$mode` contains the file permissions (see the section on `mkdir` in Chapter 2) used to create the DBM file if it doesn't exist. If you want to ensure that the file already exists, you can pass a special Perl value of `undef` for the mode.

dbmopen expands `$database` to two file names—`$database.dir` and `$database.pag`—the traditional files used by the DBM library. Thus, you provide the first part of the file name, and dbmopen provides the suffix.

After calling dbmopen, all data stored in the associative array will get written to disk into the DBM database. This preserves your data for future runs of the script. All data that were in the associative array prior to the call to dbmopen are now lost.

You store data in the associative array the same way you've always done, in the form of `$assoc{$key} = $value`.

When you're done with a DBM database, call dbmclose to close it.

```
dbmclose(%assoc)
```

You pass the associative array to dbmclose, not the database file name.

N O T E

In between the calls to dbmopen and dbmclose, all data you place in your associative array get written to disk into the DBM database.

Sometimes, the number of keys in a system DBM database can grow to huge amounts. If so, then you probably don't want to copy the entry list of keys into a Perl array using the keys function. Instead, it's a better idea to iterate over the database using the each function to extract one key/value pair at a time. See the section on associative arrays in Chapter 2 for more information.

For example, to create a DBM database, you can use the following script as a guide:

```
#
# Writing data to DBM files.
# This script makes a list of
# executable programs from a directory
# and stores the list in a DBM
# database.
#
# Usage:
```

```perl
#  Perl dbmwrite.pl directory database

$directory = $ARGV[0];
$database  = $ARGV[1];

   # Read directory.
opendir(DIR, $directory) ||
    die "Can't open \"$directory\".";

@entries = readdir(DIR);

closedir(DIR);

   # Sort results.
@sorted = sort(@entries);

print "Read $directory.\n";

   # Make DBM association.
$mode = 0666;

dbmopen(%execs, $database, $mode) or
  die "Can't open \"$database\"";

   # Process entries.
foreach $entry (@sorted) {

    print "$entry\n";

    # If file is executable, store it.
    $fullname = $directory . "/" . $entry;

    # Don't store if . or ..
    if ( ( -x $fullname ) && ($entry !~ /^\./ ) ) {

        $execs{$entry} = $fullname;
        print "Storing $entry=$fullname\n";
    }
```

```
}

# Close database.
dbmclose(%execs);

# dbmwrite.pl
```

The **dbmwrite.pl** script indexes a directory on your hard disk and stores all the executable programs in a DBM database. The name of the program is the key, and the value is the full path to the item.

You can run this script with the following parameters on UNIX:

```
perl dbmwrite.pl /usr/bin/X11 x11bin
```

This will create a DBM database called x11bin from the contents of the **/usr/bin/X11** directory (where X Window programs are stored). If a file in the directory is marked as executable (the -x $fullname test) and the file name does not start with "." (the $entry !~ /^\./ test), then the file name gets stored in the DBM database. Note the use of \. to match an actual "." rather than any non-newline character (see Chapter 4 for details on regular expression patterns).

If the **dbmwrite.pl** script completes successfully, you should see two new files in the current directory—**x11bin.dir** and **x11bin.pag**, the DBM database.

Using DBM Databases

Once we've created a DBM database, we can extract the data, again using dbmopen and dbmclose. The following **dbmread.pl** script reads in data from a given DBM database and formats a report for the output. This time, the output data get written to STDOUT, the default output on your screen.

The **dbmread.pl** script again calls dbmopen to tie the associative array to the DBM database. Then, **dbmread.pl** uses each to extract each key/value pair from the database. The write command prints out the data, using the STDOUT and STDOUT_TOP formats.

The **dbmread.pl** script follows:

```
#
# Reads DBM file, printing entries.
#
# Usage:
#   Perl dbmread.pl database

# Print format for STDOUT.
format STDOUT=
@<<<<<<<<<<<<   @<<<<<<<<<<<<<<<<<<<<<<<<<<<<<<<<<<<
$key, $value
.


format STDOUT_TOP=
Program          File Name                page @<<<
$%
.


$database  = $ARGV[0];

  # Make DBM association.
$mode = 0666;

dbmopen(%execs, $database, undef) or
  die "Can't open \"$database\"";

  # Process entries.
while ( ($key,$value) = each(%execs) ) {
    write;
}

 # Close database.
dbmclose(%execs);

# dbmread.pl
```

The **dbmread.pl** script requires the name of the DBM database, the same name given to **dbmwrite.pl**. The data are formatted as shown in the following abbreviated listing:

```
Program          File Name                    page 1
xclipboard       /usr/bin/X11/xclipboard
xsm              /usr/bin/X11/xsm
xroach           /usr/bin/X11/xroach
xv               /usr/bin/X11/xv
xcalc            /usr/bin/X11/xcalc
XF86_S3          /usr/bin/X11/XF86_S3
xprop            /usr/bin/X11/xprop
imake            /usr/bin/X11/imake
xdpyinfo         /usr/bin/X11/xdpyinfo
ghostview        /usr/bin/X11/ghostview
fvwm95-2         /usr/bin/X11/fvwm95-2
xman             /usr/bin/X11/xman
xedit            /usr/bin/X11/xedit
bitmap           /usr/bin/X11/bitmap
xmahjongg        /usr/bin/X11/xmahjongg
tkdesk           /usr/bin/X11/tkdesk
```

Notice that while the data were sorted before being written to the DBM database, the data were not stored in sorted order.

Many versions of DBM restrict the size of the data you can place into any entry, oftentimes no key or value may exceed 1K bytes. Newer versions of DBM, such as gdbm, don't suffer from these restrictions. In any case, DBM databases aren't intended for large databases such as hospital patient record databases.

Sendmail, Usenet news (for history files), and other UNIX software often use DBM databases. Perl can access these databases, but sometimes you'll find a trailing NULL character (character 0) at the end of every entry (a legacy of the C programming language). If you find your data formatted that way, you can use chop on all values read in from the database to remove the trailing NULL. You must remember to append a NULL character, "\0" in Perl, to the end of each data value you write into the database.

Using `AnyDBM_File`

Perl 5 replaces `dbmopen` and `dbmclose` with the more general-purpose functions `tie` and `untie`. The problem lies in getting `tie` to work the way you want. So, many still use Perl's `dbmopen` and `dbmclose` functions.

The `tie` function ties an associative array to some package, say a DBM package. This acts a lot like `dbmopen`. The `untie` function then removes the connection set up by `tie` and, therefore, acts a lot like `dbmclose`.

The `tie` function takes the following parameters:

```
tie(%assoc, classname, list);
```

The *classname* comes from the package you intend to use. The *list* holds any further options required by the *classname*. For example, with DBM files, you need to pass the database name and then the DBM options; see your gdbm, ndbm or DBM online manual pages for details on these options.

`untie` then removes the connection:

```
untie(%assoc);
```

The first problem in using `tie` and `untie` with DBM databases is that different packages exists for each of the DBM implementations, such as `NDBM_File`, `GDBM_File`, and `DB_File`, with `DB_File` being the most radically different. And, just about every system comes with a different underlying DBM library. Linux systems, for example, come with gdbm, while most commercial UNIX systems come with DBM or ndbm.

To deal with this issue, Perl 5 comes with a package called `AnyDBM_File`. You can use this package to connect to whatever style of DBM your system supports. However, you still have to deal with differences in the parameters passed to `tie`.

Another problem in using `tie` is the vast amount of work you need to do to get Perl's `tie` mechanism to work. See the **perltie** online documentation for more on this subject.

Connecting Other Databases to Perl

DBM databases are great for hashed lists of keys/value pairs. For serious database usage, you'll probably use a real database, such as relational databases like Oracle, Informix, and Sybase, or object databases like **Versant** or **Objectify**.

There are a number of freely available packages to help interface to all the popular databases. For example, the DBI module provides a generic database interface. Submodules connect to Oracle, Informix, and Sybase databases. For Windows, the ODBC (Open Database Connectivity) module connects Perl to any ODBC-compliant database.

CD-ROM

See the **contrib/database** directory on the accompanying CD-ROM.

Perl, combined with a database module to connect to Oracle databases and Perl CGI scripts for Web pages, make a powerful combination. Together, you can make Perl scripts that create database reports as Web pages, dramatically simplifying both your work and the user's attempts to work with your databases. See Chapter 9 for more on Perl and Web pages.

Summary

A format defines how data written to a file will appear. The format defines where the data will go and how many digits will be used.

In addition to `print` and `write`, two other commands allow you to format data for output—`printf` and `sprintf`. `sprintf` returns a formatted string, and `printf` formats a string and prints it.

`dbmopen` associates a DBM database file with a Perl associative array. You store data in the associative array the same way you've always done, in the form of `$assoc{$key}` = `$value`. When you're done with a DBM database, call `dbmclose` to close it.

Perl Commands Introduced in This Chapter

dbmclose
dbmopen
format
gmtime
localtime
tie
time
untie
write

CHAPTER 6

Launching Applications

This chapter covers:

- The `fork` and `exec` process model
- The system call
- Waiting for child processes to exit
- Creating processes on Windows
- Perl scripts as DOS batch files
- Detecting whether a script is running on Windows or UNIX
- Killing processes
- Piping data between processes
- Going to sleep and waking up with an alarm

Launching External Programs

In most scripting languages, including the DOS batch files and UNIX shell scripts, a large part of most scripts involves launching external programs. Perl, also a scripting language, provides a wealth of functions that allow you to execute and control other processes. The vast majority of these functions are based on the UNIX process model, something that's important to understand if you're more familiar with Windows than UNIX.

In UNIX, the basic means for process execution is cloning. In order to launch another process, a process must clone itself. In UNIX terminology, this is called forking, after the `fork` system call. The process conducting the fork is called the *parent process* and the cloned process is called the *child*.

But, before you think UNIX is too family-oriented, note that all children must die. fork is the main means for launching new processes on UNIX.

Of course, an operating system isn't merely clones of the same process. You need to be able to run other programs. (In UNIX, a *process* is a program that is executing in memory. A *program* is an executable file on disk. Loading the program from disk into memory and running it makes it a process.)

To run other programs, UNIX provides the exec system call. exec allows a process to overlay itself with a different program and execute that program instead. Once you call exec, the original process is gone, replaced by the new program.

By combining fork and exec, you can run almost any program. The original process forks, creating a clone. The clone then willingly commits suicide by calling exec to launch another application. The original process remains untouched; the clone exec's the other program. The new process is considered a child process. The original process is the parent. Thus, UNIX processes appear in a hierarchy.

This is how UNIX systems start up. An original process called *init* starts. The init process forks, and the clones exec other applications, brining up all the programs concurrently running on modern UNIX systems.

Based on the UNIX model, Perl provides an exec command. The exec command executes a system program and never returns:

```
exec arguments
```

You pass the command-line arguments to exec in the form of an array. If there is only one argument, a simple scalar value will suffice.

To show exec, the **exec.pl** script runs a program called xterm with the -ls command-line arguments:

```
#
# Using exec.
#

exec("xterm", "-ls");

# exec.pl
```

If you run this script on a UNIX system, you should see a new **xterm** window appear. If nothing happens, an error probably occurred. A likely error is that the system did not find the program named **xterm** to run. In this case, you may need the full path to the command:

```
exec("/usr/bin/X11/xterm", "-ls");
```

Of course, the programs that are available to execute differ between UNIX and Windows. On Windows, a more likely program is **PBRUSH.EXE**, the image-editing program, which follows:

```
#
# Using exec.
#

exec("pbrush", "CAT.BMP");

# execwin.pl
```

For this script to work, you must have a file named **CAT.BMP**. If you don't, you'll see a Windows error dialog stating that the file can't be found.

If you want to continue your Perl script after executing a program, call `system` instead of `exec`.

NOTE

If your process needs are simple, a better method for launching a subprocess is `system`.

The `system` command executes a command and waits until that command completes. In most cases, this is what you want.

```
$return_value = system(command);
```

The `$return_value` will hold an integer. You must divide this value by 256 to get the actual return value. By convention, a return value of 0 means OK.

For example, to launch the **df** (UNIX disk free) command, you can use the following script:

```
#
# Using system.
#
$return_value = system("df");

print "System returned $return_value\n";

# sys.pl
```

Calling **df** will print out data to **df**'s STDOUT file handle. After that, system will return control to your Perl script, which then calls print to display the return value from system. For example,

```
% perl sys.pl

Filesystem   1024-blocks  Used Available Capacity Mounted on
/dev/sda1    1003894      237904  714126     25%    /
System returned 0
```

On Windows, you need to run a Windows program, such as **NOTEPAD.EXE**:

```
#
# Using system.
#
$return_value = system("NOTEPAD");

print "System returned $return_value\n";

# syswin.pl
```

 On UNIX, system really creates a clone under the hood. First, your process gets cloned from the fork call. Then, the clone calls exec to launch the child subprocess. Meanwhile, the parent process—your original process—calls wait to block waiting until the child process completes (dies).

In addition to system, you can capture the output of programs using the back-tick character, `. For example,

```
#
# Using back-ticks to
# capture program output.
#
$dir = `pwd`;

print "Directory: $dir\n";

# backtick.pl
```

When you run this, you'll see output like the following:

```
Directory: /home/erc/perl/book/scripts
```

Again, you must be sure to run a program that's available on your system and actually prints out data. The **pwd** program is not part of Windows. On Windows, typing **cd** without a directory name returns the current directory:

```
#
# Using back-ticks to
# capture program output.
#
$dir = `cd`;

print "Directory: $dir\n";

# backwin.pl
```

As you can see, there are many differences in the process model and available programs on UNIX and Windows.

Launching Programs on UNIX

The basic UNIX process command is `fork`. With `fork`, you get a clone of your current process.

```
$pid = fork;
```

fork does not work on Windows.

WINDOWS

The tricky part is that both the parent and child process continue executing after the call to fork, both at the same place in your Perl script (right after the call to fork). Normally, you don't want two processes doing the same thing, so you need to be able to tell them apart. The only way to distinguish between the processes is to examine the value returned by fork. For the parent process, fork returns the process ID for the child (cloned) process. In the child process, though, fork returns 0.

So, if fork returns 0, you know that the current process is the child and not the parent. (If an error occurs, fork returns a special undefined value called undef.) For example,

```
$pid = fork;

if ($pid == 0) {
    # We're in the child process.

} elsif (! defined $pid) {
    # Not defined: means an error.
} else {
    # Parent process.
}
```

Remember that both the parent and the child are executing the same script at the same place. Normally, one or the other should diverge. The child should eventually exit or exec another process.

N O T E

When you call fork, both the parent and the child have the same open file handles. This can be a problem as both the parent's and child's data can get intermixed, if both processes print to the same file handle. It can be even more of a problem with networking socket links, such as a process's connection to the X server on UNIX. If both processes write to a socket, you'll probably experience severe problems.

WARNING

Waiting for Godot

Unless the parent process calls `wait` (or `waitpid`) to wait for the completion (termination) of the child process, your UNIX system will start having what are called zombie processes. *Zombie processes* generally don't do much damage, but they will mess up your system's process table and sometimes use CPU and other system resources. Even so, zombies are not considered a good thing. So, the proper way to fork a new process and wait for its completion is for the parent to call `wait` or `waitpid` to catch the termination of the child. This process is called *reaping*. (UNIX is full of such violent terminology.)

The `wait` command waits until a child process dies, returning the child process ID (there may be more than one). If there are no child processes, `wait` returns -1. So, you can `fork` a process using the following code snippet as a guide:

```
#
# Forking with wait to reap.
#
$pid = fork;

if ($pid == 0) {
    # We're in the child process.

    # Do something...
    print "In child.\n";

    exit(0);  # Terminate child.

} elsif (! defined $pid) {
    # Not defined: means an error.
} else {
    # Parent process.

    # Do something...

    # Reap child.
    $id = wait();
```

```
# Do something after child dies.
print "Child is dead.\n";
}
```

```
# wait.pl
```

The `waitpid` command is a bit more advanced. `waitpid` waits for a particular child process to complete, returning 1 if the process is found and -1 on
errors. To call `waitpid`, you need both the process ID of the child process
and a wait flag. This wait flag is system-dependent and, on some versions of
UNIX, may allow you to control aspects of how `waitpid` works. If you pass
a flag of 0, then `waitpid` acts much like `wait`. With this, you can use the
following code snippet to fork a child process and use `waitpid` to reap:

```
#
# Forking with waitpid to reap.
#
$pid = fork;

if ($pid == 0) {
    # We're in the child process.

    # Do something...
    print "In child.\n";

    exit(0);  # Terminate child.

} elsif (! defined $pid) {
    # Not defined: means an error.
} else {
    # Parent process.

    # Do something...
    sleep(5);  # Wait

    # Reap child.
    $status = waitpid($pid, 0);
```

```
    # Do something after child dies.
    print "Child is dead with $status.\n";
}

# waitpid.pl
```

In a simple case like this one, the child may be dead before the parent even calls waitpid. Thus, a return of -1 may not mean a bad result. In addition, not all UNIX systems support waitpid, so using wait is safer and will work on more systems.

N O T E

The POSIX module provides a slightly different version of waitpid and defines a number of process wait flags, including WNOHANG to wait without hanging. Even so, your version of UNIX may not support this. Check the online manual pages for the C functions waitpid() or wait4() to see what you system supports.

N O T E

Launching Programs on Windows

The Windows process model differs a lot from that of UNIX. And, in Windows, you should use the Win32 module to launch Windows applications.

The Win32::Process module contains a number of routines to work with Windows processes. The Create routine allows you to create (launch) a process. The basic format follows:

```
use Win32::Process;

Create($ProcessObj,
    $ApplicationName,
    $CommandLine,
    $InheritHandles,
    $CreateOptions,
    $CurrentDir);
```

The parameters to Create tend to be complicated. Create returns the $ProcessObj value, which will hold a Perl object that represents the launched process. Chapter 7 describes Perl objects. For now, though, just treat the `$ProcessObj->` syntax as though you were executing a subroutine for a particular process—the process your script launched.

The `$ApplicationName` is the full path to the executable program, such as `"C:\\WINDOWS\\NOTEPAD.EXE"` or `"C:\\PERL\\BIN\\PERL.EXE"`. Note the use of the double-backslash to insert one real backslash character into the string.

 Windows 95 tends to install the default Windows applications, like **Notepad**, in **\WINDOWS**. On Windows NT, however, this directory often has a different name, such as **\WINNT35**.

N O T E

The `$CommandLine` contains the command line as seen by the program, such as `"perl asklang.pl"` or `"NOTEPAD"`.

The `$InheritHandles` flag controls whether the process inherits handles. For most usage, a value of 0—don't inherit—will work. See the online documentation on Win32 for more information on this flag.

See the documentation likewise for the multitude of creation options for `$CreateOptions`. The two most important options include `DETACHED_PROCESS` to launch a Windows application and `CREATE_NEW_CONSOLE` to launch a Console application. Perl is a console application, whereas **Notepad** and other Windows programs are detached processes.

The `$CurrentDir` holds the current directory for the launched process. Using `"."` passes the Perl script's current directory as the launched application's current directory.

To put this all together, you can launch a Windows application like **Notepad** with the following script:

```
#
# Launch a Windows process from Win32 module.
# See online docs for more on this subject.
#
use Win32;
use Win32::Process;
```

```
#Create the process object.
Win32::Process::Create($ProcessObj,
    "C:\\WINDOWS\\NOTEPAD.EXE",
    "NOTEPAD",
    0, # Don't inherit.
    DETACHED_PROCESS,
    ".") ||   # current dir.
    die &print_error;

#Wait for the process to end. No timeout.
$ProcessObj->Wait(INFINITE) ||
    warn &print_error;

$ProcessObj->GetExitCode($ExitCode) ||
    warn &print_error;

print "Notepad exited with $ExitCode\n";

sub print_error {
    print Win32::FormatMessage( Win32::GetLastError() );
}

# winapp.pl
```

There's a number of new constructs in this example. The Win32 module (different from the Win32::Process module) contains the routines FormatMessage and GetLastError, which format an error message and return the last error code. Note that successful completion of the application does generate a code.

The warn command acts like the Perl die command, only warn just prints out a message. The online documentation for Win32::Process::Create uses the die command in place of warn in its examples, but this usage is incorrect. All usage of Wait results in an error code—even success has a code—so the script will always die at the $ProcessObj->Wait command, unless you use warn instead of die.

The $ProcessObj->Wait command waits on the given process, the process created in the script. The INFINITE flag specifies waiting until the child process dies.

The `$ProcessObj->GetExitCode` retrieves the exit code from the launched process.

When you run the preceding script, you should see the familiar **Notepad** text editor appear in a Window, as shown in Figure 6.1.

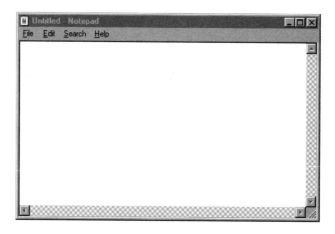

Figure 6.1 The **Notepad** application launched from Perl.

In addition to Windows applications, you can also launch text-based applications, called Console applications in Windows terminology. The following script launches our favorite Console application, Perl, using the **asklang.pl** script from Chapter 1:

```
#
# Launch a Console process from Win32 module.
# See online docs for more on this subject.
#
use Win32;
use Win32::Process;

#Create the process object.
Win32::Process::Create($ProcessObj,
    "C:\\PERL\\BIN\\PERL.EXE",
    "perl asklang.pl",
    0, # Don't inherit.
```

```
    CREATE_NEW_CONSOLE,
    ".") ||  # current dir.
    die &print_error;

#Wait for the process to end. No timeout.
$ProcessObj->Wait(INFINITE) ||
    warn &print_error;

$ProcessObj->GetExitCode($ExitCode) ||
    warn &print_error;

print "Perl exited with $ExitCode\n";

sub print_error {
    print Win32::FormatMessage( Win32::GetLastError() );
}

# winperl.pl
```

When you run this script, a new MS-DOS prompt window will appear, and the **asklang.pl** script will ask you about your favorite scripting language.

NOTE The Console application finishes as soon as the application ends. At that point, the Console window also disappears, making it very hard to see the data printed by the script. You may want to add a few commands to have the script wait until the user presses **Enter** for the script to exit. For example,

```
print "Press Enter to quit.\n";
$enter = <STDIN>;
```

Launching Perl Scripts as Batch Files

On UNIX, you can use the #!/usr/bin/perl syntax on the first line to convert a Perl script into an executable command. This means that you don't have to type **perl file.pl**; instead, you can just type **file.pl**. Windows, though, doesn't have the ability to specify the shell like UNIX. However, there's a handy utility called **pl2bat.bat**, a DOS batch file, that can convert a Perl script into a DOS batch file. This script takes advantage of both Perl and DOS syntax.

In DOS, any line beginning with REM indicates a remark, or comment, much the same as Perl's #. You can place an @ character in front of REM, and the statement still holds. Thus @REM = 'message' is a comment in DOS and an assignment in Perl.

In Perl, you can make a multiline text string. Add this fact to @REM, and you have the following code, which contains valid DOS *and* Perl syntax:

```
@rem = '
@echo off
perl -S %0.bat %1 %2 %3 %4 %5 %6 %7 %8 %9
goto endofperl
@rem ';
```

In DOS, the preceding commands call Perl, passing the *current* file with all of the command-line arguments. In Perl, the preceding commands simply set the @rem array to a very long text string. Thus, we have a part of a script that can be executed by DOS or Perl, with different results—but no errors.

With this clever notion, we can use **pl2bat.bat** to convert a Perl script to a DOS batch file. Starting with the **hello.pl** script from Chapter 1, the following command creates **hello.bat** from **hello.pl**:

```
pl2bat hello.pl
```

The original **hello.pl** script looks like the following:

```
#
# hello.pl
#
# Hello World in perl.
print "Hello World.\n";
```

The **pl2bat.bat** script then converted the Perl script into the following batch file:

```
@rem = '-*-Perl-*-';
@rem = '
@echo off
perl -S %0.bat %1 %2 %3 %4 %5 %6 %7 %8 %9
```

```
goto endofperl
@rem ';
#
# hello.pl
#
# Hello World in perl.
print "Hello World.\n";

__END__
:endofperl
```

The __END__ statement causes Perl to stop processing.

WARNING

This technique does not work on Windows 95. You need Windows NT for batch files created by **pl2bat.bat** to work.

Detecting Whether Your Script is Running on Windows or UNIX

Perl doesn't provide an easy way to determine from within your scripts which operating system your script executes on. Unfortunately, there are times, such as when launching external programs, where this information is important to know. This makes writing cross-platform scripts difficult.

Ironically, when the Perl interpreter gets compiled, it has to know this information. The **Config** module is one of the best ways of determining whether your system runs on Windows or UNIX (or OS/2 or the Macintosh, and so on).

The **Config** module gets set up when you run the **Configure** script when installing Perl. It contains a large associative array, %Config, that contains all the configuration information, most of which is useful only if you're writing new modules (see Chapter 7 for more on this topic).

The osname variable in the %Config associative array contains the name of the operating system, such as "linux" or "MSWin32". You can use this to guess which operating system your script is running under. The reason for the guess is that while you can identify Windows, because the `osname` always starts with "Windows" or "MSWin", you cannot guarantee the name of a UNIX or UNIX-like operating system. One common way to guess is that if the name has a "ux", "ix", "UX", or "IX" at the end, chances are it's a UNIX variant.

So, we can use this to guess whether a script runs under UNIX or Windows with the following script:

```
#
# Uses Config module to
# detect O.S.
#
use Config;

$os = &check_os;

print "Your O.S. is: $os\n";

#
# Uses Config module to guess O.S.
# The Config module does have the O.S.
# name, but no direct reference to UNIX,
# so you have to guess.
#
sub check_os {

    # Get O.S. name first.
    $osname = $Config{'osname'};
    $os     = "Unknown";

    # If its Windows, then it's not UNIX.
    if ( $osname =~ /^Windows/ ) {
        $os = "Windows";
    } elsif ( $osname =~ /^MSWin/ ) {
        $os = "Windows";
    #
    # Anything ending in "ux"
    # "ix", "UX" or "IX", is UNIX.
```

```
#
} elsif ( $osname =~ /ux$/ ) {
    $os = "UNIX";
} elsif ( $osname =~ /ix$/ ) {
    $os = "UNIX";
} elsif ( $osname =~ /UX$/ ) {
    $os = "UNIX";
} elsif ( $osname =~ /IX$/ ) {
    $os = "UNIX";
} else {
    # If not Windows, guess UNIX.
    # This ignores the Mac and OS/2,
    # though.
    $os = "UNIX";
}

    return $os;
}
```

config.pl

Of course, this script ignores other operating systems like OS/2, Macintosh, and AmigaOS.

If your system doesn't have the **Config** module, you can still make a good guess at the operating system by examining files on disk or environment variables. The executable name of the Perl interpreter may provide some clue. For example, if the path contains a colon or a backslash, you know its not UNIX. A value of C:\PERL\BIN\PERL.EXE in $^X, for example, clearly indicates that you're running on Windows. Even a value of "PERL.EXE" is a good clue. The current executable name of the Perl interpreter is stored in the $^X variable, so you can check that against "PERL.EXE":

```
if ($^X =~ /PERL.EXE$/) {
    $os = "Windows";
}
```

Another possible method is to check environment variables.

Checking Environment Variables

A number of environment variables are used only on UNIX, and others are only used on Windows. You can test against this in the %ENV associative array (described in Chapter 2). For example, the presence of PROMPT, USER-NAME, or HOMEDRIVE is a likely clue that the operating system is Windows. In fact, anything with a DRIVE in it is likely to be Windows, as the Windows file systems are very dependent on disk drive letters.

Similarly, USER, MANPATH, and TERM are likely on UNIX. Table 6.1 lists some common environment variables and whether you're likely to find them on UNIX or Windows.

Table 6.1 Common environment variables.

Variable	Likely On
CMDLINE	Windows.
HOMEDRIVE	Windows.
LD_LIBRARY_PATH	UNIX.
MANPATH	UNIX.
OPENWINHOME	UNIX.
OS	Windows NT, if equal to "Windows_NT".
OSTYPE	Linux (UNIX), if equal to "linux".
PROMPT	Windows.
SHELL	UNIX, but sometimes Windows.
TERM	UNIX.
USER	UNIX.
USERNAME	Windows NT.
WINDIR	Windows.

WARNING

Since you can set any environment variable you'd like, you cannot depend on these tests. In order to present a working environment on one operating system that more closely matches that of another operating system, users may set UNIX-style environment variables on Windows or Windows-style environment variables on UNIX.

Other tests include the presence of files named **/dev/null** or **/etc/utmp**, both common on UNIX, but not Windows.

There's no real way to know for sure, but your scripts can make a good guess. The following **os.pl** script contains an alternate `check_os` subroutine that you can use to check for which operating system the script runs under.

```
#
# Various tests of which operating
# system this script runs under.
#
# NO TEST IS GUARANTEED!

$os = &check_os();

print "Perl executable is $^X\n";

print "Likely O.S. is $os.\n";

#
# Subroutine you can call to check the O.S.
# Returns "Windows" for generic Windows
# of any kind, "Windows_NT" if NT, or "UNIX".
#
# Two values are kept: $os if the test
# is very likely or $likely, if the test
# is not so sure.
#
sub check_os {

    $os = "Unknown"; # Don't know yet.
    $likely_windows = "Unknown";
    $likely_unix    = "Unknown";

    # Check likely Windows ENV vars.

    if ($ENV{"PROMPT"} ne "" ) {
        $likely_windows = "Windows";
```

```perl
} elsif ($ENV{"WINDIR"} ne "" ) {
    $os = "Windows";
} elsif ($ENV{"HOMEDRIVE"} ne "" ) {
    $os = "Windows";
} elsif ($ENV{"CMDLINE"} ne "" ) {
    $likely_windows = "Windows";
} elsif ($ENV{"USERNAME"} ne "" ) {
    $likely_windows = "Windows";
} elsif ($ENV{"OS"} eq "Windows_NT" ) {
    $os = "Windows_NT";
}

# Check likely Windows ENV vars.
if ($ENV{"USER"} ne "" ) {
    $likely_unix = "UNIX";
} elsif ($ENV{"OSTYPE"} eq "linux" ) {
    $os = "UNIX";
} elsif ($ENV{"USER"} ne "" ) {
    $likely_unix = "UNIX";
} elsif ($ENV{"MANPATH"} ne "" ) {
    $likely_unix = "UNIX";
} elsif ($ENV{"TERM"} ne "" ) {
    $likely_unix = "UNIX";
} elsif ($ENV{"SHELL"} ne "" ) {
    $likely_unix = "UNIX";
} elsif ($ENV{"OPENWINHOME"} ne "" ) {
    $os = "UNIX";
} elsif ($ENV{"LD_LIBRARY_PATH"} ne "" ) {
    $os = "UNIX";
}

# Check if Perl executable is likely Windows.
if ($^X =~ /PERL.EXE$/) {
    $os = "Windows";
}

# Now resolve the differences.
if ($os ne "Unknown") {
```

```
        return $os;
    }

    if ($likely_unix ne "Unknown") {
        if ($likely_windows eq "Unknown") {
            return "UNIX";
        } else {
            # Likely both, pick Windows then.
            return "Windows";
        }
    } else {
        # Not likely UNIX, so pick Windows.
        return "Windows";
    }
}

# os.pl
```

Controlling Processes

The simplest process control command is `exit`, which exits the current
Perl script. You can pass a value to `exit`, which gets returned to the parent
process:

```
exit;
exit(value);
```

In UNIX usage, any nonzero value represents an error. Return 0 if the
process succeeded.

UNIX

To kill off a process, you need its process ID. You can then call `kill` to kill
it off:

```
kill(signal, process_id);
```

In most cases, a signal of 9 will suffice to kill the errant program:

```
kill(9, $process_id);
```

U N I X

In UNIX, kill really sends a message—a signal—to another process and nothing more. kill does not kill the process. But, if the target process has not installed a signal handler for the signal you send with kill, then the target process commits suicide. So, in most cases, kill is the smoking gun that causes another process to tip over, although kill retains plausible deniability—it wasn't directly responsible.

Pipes

A *pipe* is a UNIX concept based on the idea of piping the output of one program into the input of another. Since most things in UNIX can be treated as files, the output of one program, normally sent to STDOUT, can be used as the input for another program (normally STDIN). The pipe command, therefore, connects two file handles:

```
pipe(readhandle, writehandle);
```

All output written to the *writehandle* file gets sent to the *readhandle*. This occurrence may seem odd, but you can use it to communicate between processes. One process writes to the *writehandle*; the other reads from the *readhandle*. The data read are the same data that were written out.

One problem is how both processes get the proper file handles if the pipe is called from within one process. This is where fork comes in. Call pipe before calling fork. Then, the child and parent processes each have access to both file handles.

But, since it is a very bad idea to try to mix access to file handles, the parent and child each call close on the file handle that will not be used. Each process uses only one file handle, making the communication one way. (See Chapter 11 for numerous methods for two-way communication.)

You can try this in action with the following script:

```
#
# Using pipe and fork on UNIX.
#

pipe(FROM_CHILD, TO_PARENT);

$pid = fork;

if ($pid == 0) {
   # We're in the child process.

   # Close file handle we won't use.
   close(FROM_CHILD);

   # Send data to parent.
   print TO_PARENT "Hello, parent\n";

   exit(0);   # Terminate child.

} elsif (undef $pid) {
   # Not defined: means an error.
} else {
   # Parent process.

   # Close file handle we won't use.
   close(TO_PARENT);

   # Get data from child.
   $data = <FROM_CHILD>;
   print "From child: $data\n";

   # Reap child.
   $id = wait();

   # Do something after child dies.
   print "Child is dead.\n";
}

# pipe.pl
```

You can also open a pipe using the open command. If you use a pipe character, |, as the first character of a file name, Perl will interpret this as an attempt to open a pipe to that program. All data written to that file handle gets sent to the command line used in the call to open.

For example, to send an email message, using the UNIX **mail** command, you can use the following script:

```
#
# Using a pipe to send mail.
#
open (MAIL, "| mail erc");

print MAIL ("System build has finished\n");

close(MAIL);

# mail.pl
```

Alarm Clocks and Sleeping

The sleep command puts your process to sleep for a number of seconds:

```
sleep $seconds
```

Why would you ever want to do that? Well, you may be waiting for something else to complete, although wait and waitpid might be better for this task. One common use for sleep is for scripts that perform a task every hour or minute or other interval. You can call sleep for the desired interval. After the requisite number of seconds (at least that many seconds, but don't depend on the exact amount, as your process may oversleep if the system is busy), your process wakes up and continues on.

If you don't pass a value to sleep, your process sleeps forever. In normal practice, you use this form of sleep only if you've previously set up an alarm to later wake up your process.

An alarm is a UNIX concept. Your process asks the operating system to send an alarm signal (SIGALARM) back to your process after a certain time. When the alarm goes off, your process wakes up, in the alarm signal handler routine.

To try this out, the **alarm.pl** script creates a 5-second alarm:

```
#
# Use of alarm and signal
# handlers.
#

# Set up alarm handler.
$SIG{ALRM} = \&wakeup;

# Set alarm clock.
alarm(5);

sleep;   # Forever.

sub wakeup {

    print "Wake up!\n";
    exit(0);
}

# alarm.pl
```

The %SIG associative array contains a set of signal-handling subroutines. The \& syntax allows you to specify the name of the subroutine as a reference. See Chapter 7 for details.

The alarm call sets up a 5-second alarm. After 5 seconds (or so), the wakeup subroutine will get called. After calling alarm, the script goes to sleep forever (or until a signal arrives).

Alarms are notoriously inaccurate.

N O T E

Using `eval` to Control the Command Line

The `eval` command allows you to evaluate—or execute—a snippet of Perl code, as if it were a small Perl program itself; for example,

```
eval("print \"Hello World\n\";" );
```

Summary

Perl, originally built on top of UNIX, provides a plethora of ways to launch and control processes. The `exec` command overlays your process with that of another program. The `system` command executes an external program and then returns. The `fork` command clones your Perl script, with both the parent and child (clone) executing the same script at the same place. `fork` works only on UNIX.

If you're concerned about cross-platform scripts, `eval` and `system` work on Windows and UNIX. Most other methods work only on one or the other.

The `eval` command evaluates its parameters as a mini Perl script.

Perl Commands Introduced in This Chapter

```
eval
exit
fork
pipe
system
wait
waitpid
Win32::Process::Create
```

CHAPTER 7

Perl Packages and Modules

This chapter covers:

- Packages
- Modules
- Extensions
- Common modules and extensions
- The English module for normal variable names
- Using OLE automation on Windows
- Perl's object-oriented syntax

Packages

A *package* provides a convenient means for collecting a set of related Perl subroutines. You can use packages to help organize your Perl scripts and to make it easier to reuse subroutines in different applications. In addition, many people have already written Perl packages, so that you can use packages to reuse scripts developed by others and save yourself the time in writing everything from scratch. This chapter briefly introduces packages and modules and then shows how to use some of the more common Perl modules. The syntax for working with subroutines and data in modules differs from that of basic Perl, and you'll need to know how to use modules to work on advanced topics in Perl, such as creating CGI scripts for Web pages.

180

Perl's packages also offer a way to prevent global variables and subroutine names from stomping on each other. A package presents its own protected name space, so that a variable named $line in one package remains different from a $line variable in another package.

The Perl syntax for accessing a variable inside a package is $package::variable. You call subroutines in a package using a similar syntax, such as Win32::GetLastError() introduced in Chapter 6. You can nest packages within packages to create a hierarchy of related subroutines, such as Win32::Process::Create cited in Chapter 6. Everything in Perl, in fact, resides in a package. All the scripts developed so far are considered part of the package named main that Perl automatically creates for you.

Modules

A Perl *module* is simply a package that follows stricter guidelines and was designed to be reused. Most modules get installed into a Perl library directory, such as **C:\PERL\LIB** or **/usr/lib/perl5**. The module Perl scripts are stored in files ending in *.pm*. For modules nested within other modules, such as File::Basename, you'll see a subdirectory named **File** and inside the subdirectory, a file named **Basename.pm**.

The use command, which has already been introduced, allows you to use a module. You can also use the require command, which is quite similar to use. With require, you must always use the ModuleName::subroutine syntax. The use command allows you to pretend the subroutines and variables in the module are part of your current script, so you don't need the ModuleName:: part and can just use the subroutine and variable names alone. The use command also preloads the module and executes the BEGIN section of the module—see the section entitled "Inside a Package."

Extensions

Extensions are enhanced packages that require extra C code to provide their functionality. For example, the ODBC package for Windows is really an extension in that it adds extra functions written in C that the Perl package invokes. On systems that support dynamic loading, Perl can load in the C code at run time in the form of a dynamic or shared library.

Common Packages, Modules, and Extensions

The Perl community remains rather lax about the precise definition and usage of package, module, and extension, so don't be surprised if one is called the other. In the end, it doesn't really matter as all sorts of wonderful people have worked to provide you with extra code for your Perl scripts, and that's rather nice, whatever the code collections get called.

Among the common modules, you'll find those listed in Table 7.1.

Table 7.1 Perl 5 standard modules.

Module	Usage
AnyDBM_File	Framework for DBM access.
AutoLoader	Only load functions on demand.
AutoSplit	Splits packages for autoloading.
Benchmark	For timing code execution.
Carp	Warns of errors.
Config	Accesses Perl's configuration.
Cwd	Gets working directory.
DB_File	Accesses Berkeley UNIX DB databases.
Devel::SelfStubber	Generates stubs for self-loading modules.
diagnostics	Perl produces enhanced diagnostics.
DynaLoader	Dynamically loads C functions into Perl for extensions.
English	Provides English names for odd variables, like $_.
Env	Accesses environment variables.

Exporter	Controls import and export of modules.
ExtUtils::Liblist	Determines libraries.
ExtUtils::MakeMaker	Creates Makefile for extension.
ExtUtils::Manifest	Writes out a **MANIFEST** file for an extension.
ExtUtils::Mkbootstrap	Bootstrapping for DynaLoader.
Fcntl	Defines from **fcntl.h**.
File::Basename	Parses file names.
File::CheckTree	Checks a directory tree.
File::Find	Finds entries in directory tree.
FileHandle	Object-oriented file routines.
File::Path	Works with directories.
Getopt::Long	For command-line argument processing.
Getopt::Std	For command-line argument processing.
I18N::Collate	String comparison for multiple languages.
integer	Use integer numerics, rather than floating-point.
IPC::Open2	Open for both reading and writing.
IPC::Open3	Open for reading, writing, and handling errors.
Net::Ping	Checks another host on the network.
NT	Windows NT–specific extensions.
OLE	Windows extension for OLE automation.
POSIX	UNIX-like functions for Perl.
SelfLoader	Loads functions on demand.
Safe	Used to evaluate Perl commands in a safe environment.
Socket	Used for networking.
strict	Restricts unsafe constructs.
subs	Allows predeclaration of subroutine names.
Test::Harness	Runs standard Perl tests.
Text::Abbrev	For text abbreviations.
Win32	A set of Windows extensions.

Many of these modules are intended as aids for module writers such as `ExtUtils::Manifest` and `Exporter`. Other modules, like `Env` and `FileHandle`, replace and enhance functions already in Perl.

The supported modules on your system are stored in the Perl library directory. To find this directory—or directories—print out the `@INC` array:

```
print "@INC\n";
```

This will print out the location of the Perl library directory, such as **/usr/lib/perl5** or **C:\PERL\LIB**. Perl's modules reside in the directories named in `@INC` and have file names ending in *.pm*. To list all these files, try the following script:

```
#
# Uses glob to find all installed Perl
# modules.
#

# Copy INC, because we plan to modify list.
@dir_list = @INC;

$i = 0;
while ($i <= $#dir_list) {

    $dir = $dir_list[$i];

    &check_dir($dir);

    $i++;
}

sub check_dir {
    my($dir) = $_[0];
    my(@list);
    my($new_dir);
    my($filename);

    if ($dir eq ".") {
```

```
        return;
    }

    chdir( $dir );

    @list = glob("\*");

    foreach $filename (@list) {

        if ($filename =~ /pm$/ ) {
            print "$dir/$filename\n";
        }

        # Check if is directory.
        if ( -d $filename ) {

            $new_dir = $dir . "/" . $filename;

            # Append directory name onto dir list.
            $pos = $#dir_list + 1;

            $dir_list[$pos] = $new_dir;
        }
    }
}

# module.pl
```

Instead of the **module.pl** script, you can use the UNIX **find** command to find all the module files in the Perl library directory:

U N I X find `perl -e 'print "@INC"'` -name '*.pm' -print

If you use **module.pl** or **find**, you'll see a list like the following:

```
/usr/lib/perl5/AnyDBM_File.pm
/usr/lib/perl5/AutoLoader.pm
/usr/lib/perl5/AutoSplit.pm
```

```
/usr/lib/perl5/Benchmark.pm
/usr/lib/perl5/Carp.pm
/usr/lib/perl5/Cwd.pm
/usr/lib/perl5/English.pm
```

The rest of the chapters in this book will introduce useful Perl modules. Two modules of note, though, include the English and OLE automation modules.

The English Module

Perl seems particularly prone to odd variables names like $^X and $'. To help you deal with this, Perl offers the English module, which ties the odd-named variables into something more understandable. If you place the use English; command in your scripts, you can use the longer variables names. Table 7.2 lists the punctuation variables and their corresponding long names. You'll notice that just about all the punctuation available has been used to good effect.

Table 7.2 Some special global variables in Perl.

Variable	English	Usage
$^A	$ACCUMULATOR	Current value of write accumulator for format data.
$_	$ARG	Default input and pattern-searching variable.
$^T	$BASETIME	Time script began running in time format.
$?	$CHILD_ERROR	Status returned by last pipe close or system function.
$^D	$DEBUGGING	Current value of Perl's debugging flags.
$)	$EFFECTIVE_GROUP_ID	Effective group ID for the Perl process. setgid may change this.

`$>`	`$EFFECTIVE_USER_ID`	Effective user ID of process.
`$^X`	`$EXECUTABLE_NAME`	Name of Perl binary, e.g., **PERL.EXE** or **perl**.
`$!`	`$ERRNO`	If numeric context, holds errno result of math function; if string context, holds error message.
`$@`	`$EVAL_ERROR`	Error message from last `eval` call.
`$^L`	`$FORMAT_FORMFEED`	Output to advance a page from `write`.
`$:`	`$FORMAT_LINE_BREAK_CHARACTERS`	Characters allowed to break on when filling continuation fields in a format.
`$-`	`$FORMAT_LINES_LEFT`	Number of lines left on current page.
`$=`	`$FORMAT_LINES_PER_PAGE`	Total number of lines available on page.
`$~`	`$FORMAT_NAME`	Name of current format.
`$%`	`$FORMAT_PAGE_NUMBER`	Page number in current format.
`$^`	`$FORMAT_TOP_NAME`	Name of top-of-page format.
`$.`	`$INPUT_LINE_NUMBER`	Line number in the last file handle that was read.
`$/`	`$INPUT_RECORD_SEPARATOR`	Ends a line of text for input, newline on UNIX, carriage return and newline on Windows.
`$+`	`$LAST_PAREN_MATCH`	Last bracket matched by last search.
`$"`	`$LIST_SEPARATOR`	Output field separator for elements of an array; defaults to a space.
`$&`	`$MATCH`	String matched by last match.

$#	$OFMT	Output format for numbers printed with print (not using the `format` command described in Chapter 5). Normally %.20g.
$|	$OUTPUT_AUTOFLUSH	If non-zero forces a flush with each write or print
$,	$OUTPUT_FIELD_SEPARATOR	Output field separator.
$\	$OUTPUT_RECORD_SEPARATOR	Output record separator, equivalent of $/ for output.
$]	$PERL_VERSION	String printed by `perl -v`; version number.
$'	$POSTMATCH	String following last match.
$`	$PREMATCH	String preceding last match.
$$	$PROCESS_ID	The process ID for this script.
$0	$PROGRAM_NAME	Name of current Perl script.
$(	$REAL_GROUP_ID	Group ID for the Perl process.
$<	$REAL_USER_ID	Real user ID.
$^F	$SYSTEM_FD_MAX	Maximum system file descriptor.
$^W	$WARNING	True if warning is turned on (by perl -w); False otherwise

There are even more global variables than listed in Table 7.2. See the online documentation on **perlvar** for more information. Don't worry; you're not likely to need to modify the vast majority of these variables.

OLE Automation

Object Linking and Embedding (OLE) forms a powerful way for Windows applications to communicate and control each other. A Perl script can, for example, invoke OLE-supporting applications, like Microsoft's Excel or Word, place data in the application and cause the application to save the data to a file or print it out. This makes a very handy way for Perl to act as the master control for a set of operations on common Windows software.

Once you start researching it, you'll find OLE to be a daunting subject. There's a huge amount of material you need to know. Perl hides a lot of the messy details with the OLE module.

The OLE module allows you to create OLE objects that represent Windows applications. You can send OLE messages to the objects and ask the applications to perform all sorts of tasks.

To use the OLE module, you need to execute the use command:

```
use OLE;
```

To do much of anything, you also need to create an OLE object from some existing application, such as Microsoft Excel. The OLE object represents the Windows application in your Perl script. In fact, creating an OLE object in Perl will launch the application. To launch Microsoft Excel, for example, you can use the following code:

```
$app = CreateObject OLE "Excel.Application" ||
    die "Unable to open Excel.";
```

The value returns $app, which now contains a Perl OLE object. You use this object to interact, via OLE, with the application represented by $app in Excel.

Once you have created an OLE object, you can start sending it messages. Messages sent to the Perl object get forwarded on to the application by the subroutines in the OLE module. These messages allow you to control the application, Excel in this case.

The main problem is discovering what messages to send. One of the best sources of information is Visual Basic, because it's fairly easy to convert Visual Basic syntax to Perl. For examples of this conversion, look in the **eg** subdirectory underneath the main directory where you installed Perl for Win32, such as **\PERL**.

It's way beyond the scope of this book to cover the intricacies of OLE (see Appendix A for a listing of books to help with OLE). But, you can use the following example script, which controls Excel, as a guide in writing your own OLE automation scripts:

```
#
# Use OLE to control MS Excel.
#
use OLE;

# Create an instance of Excel.
$app = CreateObject OLE "Excel.Application" ||
    die "Unable to open Excel.";

# Make application visible.
$app->{'Visible'} = 1;

# Create a new workbook.
$app->Workbooks->Add();

# Set values in a "range".
$app->Range("A1")->{'Value'} = "Developer";
$app->Range("B1")->{'Value'} = "Bugs";

$app->Range("B2")->{'Value'} = "Assigned";
$app->Range("C2")->{'Value'} = "Fixed";

$app->Range("A3")->{'Value'} = "Eric J.";
$app->Range("B3")->{'Value'} = 10;
$app->Range("C3")->{'Value'} = 10;

# Leave Excel running. Use $app->Quit() to exit.

# msexcel.pl
```

Just about everyone uses Excel as an example because it's a commonly available application that supports OLE quite well. The preceding script creates an OLE object that launches Excel. The $app->{'Visible'} = 1; command uses Perl's object-oriented syntax to set a value (1) into a hidden associative array that is referenced from the application object. This makes Excel appear on the screen.

The Workbooks->Add() subroutine adds a new workbook (the basic document type in Excel). The Range subroutine references a range of values (in the preceding usage, a range of one value). You can quit Excel by calling the `Quit` subroutine.

When you run this script, you'll see a small spreadsheet like the one in Figure 7.1.

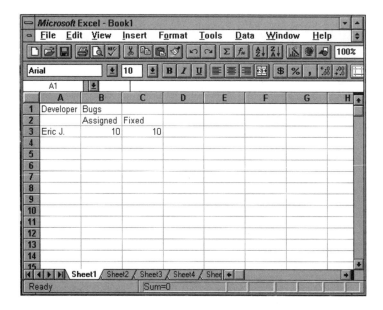

Figure 7.1 Creating an Excel spreadsheet from Perl.

See the **oleauto** online documentation for more on using OLE automation from Perl.

Inside a Package

Two special subroutines are inside a package. The `BEGIN` subroutine gets executed as soon as possible upon any use of a package. The `END` subroutine gets executed as late as possible, usually when your script is exiting. You can have more than one `BEGIN` or `END` subroutines; they get executed in order.

The use *ModuleName* command explicitly executes the BEGIN statements in that module.

The purpose of BEGIN and END is to allow for initialization and clean-up code for a package. This enables the package to set everything up for easy use by you.

Subroutine Prototypes

Perl 5.002 also offers what are called *subroutine prototypes*. With prototypes, you can specify the parameters that a subroutine expects. Unfortunately, the current version only allows bizarre punctuation to define the prototypes. Future versions of Perl should add fully named prototypes, where you provide the names of all the parameters passed to a subroutine. For now, unless you're writing modules, it's best to stay away from these subroutine prototypes.

Perl for Win32 remains at Perl 5.001, not 5.002, as of this writing.

WINDOWS

References and Objects

A *reference* is a scalar variable in Perl that points—or refers to—something else. This is very useful in setting up a Perl associative array to hold subroutines to call and so on. References often hide data—purposely—so that you don't have to worry about the messy details "behind the curtain." The Win32 module used in Chapter 6 used references to hide implementation details about Win32 processes, details you normally don't want to have to deal with.

References are fairly advanced topics, so this section will merely introduce them and refer you to the **perlref** online documentation for more information. References are used extensively in modules, so you need to at least know the basics.

To set up a reference, you use a backslash character before the name of what you're referring to. For example, to set up a reference from one scalar variable to another, you can use the following syntax:

```
$reference = \$referred_to;
```

The same syntax works for arrays and associative arrays, as shown here:

```
$arrayref  = \@ARGV;
$assocref  = \%ENV;
```

You can also set up a reference to a subroutine:

```
$subref = \&subroutine;
```

The purpose of such references is to allow a variable to specify a subroutine to execute.

To access a reference, you need to remember that the reference is a scalar variable. So, to access the referred-to array, use the @ to specify an array and the scalar variable, which begins with a $. Examples of this syntax follow:

```
#
# Using references.
#

$var = "Hello";

$reference = \$var;
$arrayref  = \@ARGV;
$assocref  = \%ENV;
$subref    = \&sub1;

print "Scalar reference = $$reference\n";

@sorted = sort( @$arrayref );
print "Array  reference = @sorted\n";
```

```
while ( ($key, $value) = each( %$assocref ) ) {

    print "Assoc. ref $key=$value\n";
}
```

```
print "Call a subroutine via references.\n";
&$subref(10);

sub sub1 {
    my($param) = $_[0];

    print "In a subroutine with $param.\n";
}


# ref.pl
```

Object-Oriented Scripting

Object-oriented languages such as Java and C++ have captured the computing industry by storm. Perl also supports a primitive version of objects and
methods (subroutines called to act on an object) by using references.

When you see the -> operator (taken from C++), you know that a
method (subroutine) is being called on an object (reference variable). For
example, in Chapter 6's section on Win32 process creation, the
Win32::Process::Create subroutine stored an object (really a reference
to data) in the $ProcessObj variable. Later on, the **winapp.pl** script called
the GetExitCode method on the $ProcessObj variable, using code like
the following:

```
$ProcessObj->GetExitCode($ExitCode);
```

Under the hood, the -> syntax acts more like traditional Perl, something
like the following:

```
&GetExitCode($ProcessObj, $ExitCode);
```

Also borrowed from C++ is the idea of a new function that acts as an object "constructor." new is simply a subroutine in a package that creates a new object and returns a reference to that object to your code.

194

There's really more to it than this, but this is the simplest way to look at Perl objects. See the **perlobj** online documentation for more information on this complex subject.

To use a package that provides objects like the Win32 package in Chapter 6 or **Perl/Tk** in Chapter 12, you simply need to follow the examples given.

Summary

A package provides a convenient means for collecting a set of related Perl subroutines. You can use packages to help organize your Perl scripts and make it easier to reuse subroutines in different applications.

A Perl module is simply a package that follows stricter guidelines and was designed to be reused. Most modules get installed into a Perl library directory, such as **C:\PERL\LIB** or **/usr/lib/perl5**.

Extensions are enhanced packages that require extra C code to provide their functionality.

A reference is a scalar variable in Perl that points—or refers to—something else. To set up a reference, you use a backslash character before the name of what you're referring to.

Perl Commands Introduced in This Chapter

OLE::CreateObject

Advanced Perl

This section builds on the basics introduced so far and extends the use of Perl into more practical domains. In the remaining chapters, you'll apply the basic Perl skills introduced in the first seven chapters and add Perl to your practical problem-solving toolbox.

Chapter 8 covers using Perl for system administration tasks. While it's hard to nail down what exactly system administrators must do—since their jobs are constantly changing—this chapter focuses on frequent tasks like user management.

Chapter 9 tackles the hot topic of using Perl for creating dynamic Web pages. Perl is ideal for interfacing with databases and handling data-entry forms in Web pages. It's also great fun to be able to see your work appear on a Web page.

Chapter 10 provides a lot of ideas for handling cross-platform software development. Since Perl runs on Windows and UNIX systems, you can use Perl to help automate your software build tasks.

Chapter 11 handles client-server issues with Perl. It's amazing, but Perl contains a huge number of networking commands built into the core language. You can create network daemons in Perl and facilitate client-server data exchange.

Chapter 12 ends the book with a bang, showing you how to create graphical interfaces for your Perl scripts using the **Perl/TK** extension.

## CHAPTER 8

Perl for System Administration

This chapter covers:

- Working with users and extracting user names
- UNIX password file data
- Host names
- System information on Windows
- The Windows registry

Working with Users

An administrator's job is never done, especially with those pesky beings called users. Perl offers a lot of facilities for aiding administrators. Perl helps with

- Parsing complicated administration files so that you can automatically add users to groups and so on.
- Reporting on system status.
- Turning on and off system services.

You'll find that system administration becomes the area where Perl diverges the most between operating systems. This isn't Perl's fault; it's really the operating systems that are different, forcing Perl to become different. Even so, with its ability to launch and control processes, manipulate files, and parse text, Perl is ideal for many system administration tasks. This chapter provides an overview of Perl commands and modules of special interest to system administrators.

Login Names

Most users have a login name, and it's very common to access and manipulate user records based on their login names. The getlogin function returns a user's login name:

```
#
# Gets user login name.
#
$username = getlogin();

print "User name: $username\n";

# getlogin.pl
```

getlogin should work on both UNIX and Windows. Many other user-related functions don't.

On Windows, there's also the Win32::LoginName function:

WINDOWS

```
#
# Gets user login name on Windows.
#
use Win32;

$username = Win32::LoginName();

print "User name: $username\n";

# winlogin.pl
```

UNIX Password File Data

On UNIX, the **/etc/passwd** file traditionally stored information about each user allowed on the system. In modern times, this information may be found instead in a shadow password file (e.g., hidden elsewhere by the system) or distributed over a network by NIS (Network Information System, formerly called Yellow Pages) or some other networking scheme.

For all these cases, the `getpwnam` function retrieves a password entry for a given user name, returning a list of user data. The values returned come from the traditional definition of entries in the UNIX **/etc/passwd** file and are listed in Table 8.1.

Table 8.1 Values returned by getpwnam.

Value	Contains
`$name`	User name.
`$passwd`	Encrypted password.
`$uid`	User ID.
`$gid`	Group ID.
`$quota`	Allowed disk quota, often used for other purposes.
`$comment`	Generally unused.
`$gcos`	Often contains full user name.
`$dir`	User's home directory.
`$shell`	Program that gets launched for the user as the login shell.

Perl's `getpwnam` function uses the UNIX system call `getpwnam()`, which—on most systems at least—should take care of all the different possible locations. Thus, treat all references to **/etc/passwd** as a generic identifier for all the possible locations for user account information.

Neither `getpwnam` nor `getpwent` works on Windows.

WINDOWS

You can use the following example for calling `getpwnam`:

```
($name, $passwd, $uid,
 $gid, $quota, $comment,
 $gcos, $dir, $shell) = getpwnam($username);
```

For example, to display all the **/etc/passwd** fields for a number of users (passed on the command line), you can use the following script:

```
#
# UNIX call to getpwnam.
#

foreach $username (@ARGV) {

    ($name, $passwd, $uid,
     $gid, $quota, $comment,
     $gcos, $dir, $shell) = getpwnam($username);

    print "name    = $name\n";
    print "passwd  = $passwd\n";
    print "uid     = $uid\n";
    print "gid     = $gid\n";
    print "quota   = $quota\n";
    print "comment = $comment\n";
    print "gcos    = $gcos\n";
    print "dir     = $dir\n";
    print "shell   = $shell\n\n";
}

# getpwnam.pl
```

When you run this script, pass in the user names for which you want information on the command line, as shown next:

```
perl getpwnam.pl erc kevin
```

You'll see output like the following:

```
name    = erc
passwd  = XHsThaB8/mmMA5ERgJuf
uid     = 501
gid     = 100
quota   =
comment =
gcos    = Eric F. Johnson
dir     = /home/erc
shell   = /bin/csh

name    = kevin
passwd  = HkTsi/3pGMZ1k
uid     = 502
gid     = 100
quota   =
comment =
gcos    = Kevin Reichard
dir     = /home/kevin
shell   = /bin/bash
```

In addition to getpwnam, you can call getpwuid, which gets user information from a UNIX user ID rather than a user name. getpwuid returns the same data.

If you don't know a user name or UID in advance, you can use getpwent (short for get password entry) to iterate through the entire user list.

getpwent returns an entry for each user in **/etc/passwd**, a list of the same data as shown in Table 8.1. You can print out all users on your UNIX system with the following script:

```
#
# Print info on all users
# of a UNIX system.
#

while ( ($name, $passwd, $uid,
    $gid, $quota, $comment,
```

```
        $gcos, $dir, $shell) = getpwent ) {

    print "name    = $name\n";
    print "passwd  = $passwd\n";
    print "uid     = $uid\n";
    print "gid     = $gid\n";
    print "quota   = $quota\n";
    print "comment = $comment\n";
    print "gcos    = $gcos\n";
    print "dir     = $dir\n";
    print "shell   = $shell\n\n";
}

# allusers.pl
```

If you run this script, you'll see a lot of odd users like `ftp`, `guest`, `uucp`, `games`, `man`, `operator`, `postmaster`, `bin`, `daemon`, `adm`, `lp`, `sync`, `halt`, `mail`, `news`, and my favorite, `nobody`. These are administrative accounts.

Perl provides a number of other UNIX functions to access user and group IDs. See the online documentation on **perlfunc** for more information.

HostNames

The standard way to get a system's network or host name is via the `Sys::Hostname` module:

```
#
# Get system host name.
#

use Sys::Hostname;

$host = hostname;
```

```
print "Network host name is: $host\n";
```

```
# hostname.pl
```

203

The hostname subroutine attempts a number of different ways to get the system's hostname, none of which work on Windows. For Windows, try Win32::NodeName and Win32::DomainName, which are illustrated later.

WINDOWS

Windows System Information

Many of the UNIX-derived Perl functions simply don't work on Windows. Luckily, the Win32 module provides a large number of Windows-specific functions to help you.

The following script calls a number of the subroutines in the Win32 module to extract information about your system:

```
#
# Get information on a
# Windows system.
#
use Win32;

#
# Networking info.
#
$node   = Win32::NodeName;
$domain = Win32::DomainName;

#
# File system.
#
$fstype = Win32::FsType;
$cwd    = Win32::GetCwd;
```

```
#
# Operating System.
#
@os   = Win32::GetOSVersion;
$isnt = Win32::IsWinNT;
$is95 = Win32::IsWin95;

# Perl
$perlvers = Win32::PerlVersion;

# Print info.
print "Node=$node, Domain=$domain\n";

print "File System=$fstype\n";
print "Current directory=$cwd\n";

print "Windows version $os[1]\.$os[2] Build $os[3]\n";

if ($isnt) {
    print "Running Windows NT\n";
}

if ($is95) {
    print "Running Windows 95\n";
}
print "Perl version=$perlvers\n";

# wininfo.pl
```

When you run this script, you'll see values like the following:

```
Node=YONSEN, Domain=<YONSEN>
File System=FAT
Current directory=C:\erc\books\perl\testing
Windows version 4.0 Build 67109814
Running Windows 95
Perl version=Build 106
```

The Windows Registry

You can also access the Windows registry from the `Win32::Registry` module. The *registry* is the place on Windows where applications are supposed to register information about themselves. Window applications store persistent state information in the registry. In Windows 95 and NT, the registry replaces the state information that used to reside in **.INI** files.

While the registry itself is beyond the scope of this book (see Appendix A for a list of Windows books), the two most useful subroutines in the `Win32::Registry` module are `Open` and `GetKeys`.

The `Open` subroutine opens a key in the registry and creates a Perl object that allows you to access that key. Keys in the Windows registry are stored hierarchically, so that you'll probably have to call `Open` on a top-level key (such as `"SOFTWARE"`) and then go down the tree of names, opening each in turn, until you find the key you're really interested in.

To help you get started, and since you must call `Open` on some Perl object, the `Win32::Registry` module predefines a number of objects you can use to traverse the registry. These predefined objects include:

- `$HKEY_LOCAL_MACHINE`
- `$HKEY_USERS`
- `$HKEY_CURRENT_USER`
- `$HKEY_CLASSES_ROOT`

WARNING The online documentation for most of these subroutines is incorrect. To find the correct usage, you need to examine the Perl module, stored in the **Registry.pm** file in the **lib\Win32** directory, underneath your top-level Perl directory, for example, **C:\perl\lib\Win32**.

The `Open` subroutine, called from a Perl object, requires two parameters: the name of the key to open and a Perl variable to hold the object created for that key. For example,

```
use Win32::Registry;
$HKEY_LOCAL_MACHINE->Open("SOFTWARE",
```

```
$hkey) or
die "Can't open registry";
```

The preceding example opens the top-level key named "SOFTWARE" on the current (local) machine. If it completes successfully, then you can use the $hkey variable as a reference to a Perl object and call Open on it. For example,

```
$hkey->Open("Microsoft",
    $mkey) or
    die "Can't open registry";
```

This is how you traverse down the list of keys in the registry hierarchy. Of course, the first problem is finding the names of the keys. Once you've opened a key in the registry, you can call GetKeys to get all the keys underneath that object. For example:

```
$HKEY_LOCAL_MACHINE->Open("SOFTWARE",
    $hkey) or
    die "Can't open registry";

$hkey->GetKeys($key_list);
```

The value stored in $key_list is a reference to a Perl array (see Chapter 7). Thus, to access the array elements, you need to use the @$key_list syntax like the following:

```
foreach $key (@$key_list) {

    print "$key\n";
}
```

Since a necessary starting task is to find the keys in your system's registry, the following script extracts the key names of all the items in the registry for your local machine, under the general category of "SOFTWARE":

```
#
# Access Windows registry.
#
use Win32::Registry;
```

```perl
#
# Must open first key from
# a predefined key, like the
# local machine. See Registry.pm
# for more on this.
#
$HKEY_LOCAL_MACHINE->Open("SOFTWARE",
    $hkey) or
    die "Can't open registry";

$hkey->GetKeys($key_list);

print "SOFTWARE keys\n";
foreach $key (@$key_list) {

    print "$key\n";
    &extract_keys($hkey, $key, 0);
}

# Prints spaces to indent.
sub print_spaces {
    my($spaces) = $_[0];

    for ($i = 0; $i < $spaces; $i++) {
        print " ";
    }
}

#
# Extracts subkeys of an item
# in the registry.
#
sub extract_keys {
    my($hkey)   = $_[0];
    my($name)   = $_[1];
    my($spaces) = $_[2];
    my($newkey);
    my($key_list);
```

```
    my($key);

    $hkey->Open($name, $newkey);

    $newkey->GetKeys($key_list);

    # Print keys and extract subkeys
    &print_spaces($tabs);
    foreach $key (@$key_list) {
        if ($key ne "" ) {
            &print_spaces($spaces);
            print " $key\n";
            &extract_keys($newkey, $key, $spaces+2);
        }
    }
}
# registry.pl
```

N O T E The extract_keys subroutine in the **registry.pl** script shows the first example of a subroutine calling itself. This is called *recursion*. You need to be careful about recursion, so that the subroutine does not recur forever; there must be some terminating condition, or Perl will generate a run-time exception.

When you run the **registry.pl** script, you'll see a lot of interesting entries in your system's registry, such as the following:

```
Internet Explorer
    Styles
    Document Caching
    Image Caching
    Main
    PageSetup
    SecurityProtocols
Resource Kit
    PERL5
Shared Tools Location
```

```
New User Settings
  Word
    7.0
      Options
      Proofing Tools
      Hyphenate
        1033
          Normal
        2057
          Normal
        3081
          Normal
      Help
        Files
      Text Converters
        Import
          SPLUS
          MSPAB
```

The Win32 module supports a number of subroutines for networking, covered in Chapter 11, and some subroutines for Windows NT only. For more on the Win32 modules, see the **win32mod** online documentation. For more on the Windows registry, see *Programming Windows 95*, mentioned in Appendix A.

Other Administration Tasks

Since quite a lot of system administrators, especially UNIX administrators, use Perl extensively, you'll find a lot of modules available for helping with many tasks. The Quota module, for instance, helps manage user disk quotas. A huge number of other modules are available.

CD-ROM

Look for the **modlist.htm** file in the **doc** directory of the CD-ROM. This contains a list of many Perl modules and information on how to retrieve them. Many of these modules reside on the CD-ROM. Modules of aid to administrators reside in the **contrib/admin** directory.

Summary

While all Perl is helpful for system administrators, this chapter focuses on some specific functions and subroutines of special use for administrators.

Among these, the getlogin function gets the user's login name.

On UNIX, you can use the getpwent, getpwnam, and getpwuid functions to extract information from the **/etc/passwd** file, which holds user account information.

The Win32 module contains a large number of subroutines for acquiring information on Windows, including Win32::FsType, Win32::NodeName, and Win32::GetOSVersion.

You can use the Win32::Registry module to extract and modify information in the Windows registry.

Perl Commands Introduced in This Chapter

```
getlogin
getpwent
getpwnam
getpwuid
Win32::DomainName
Win32::FsType
Win32::GetCwd
Win32::GetOSVersion
Win32::IsWin95
Win32::IsWinNT
Win32::NodeName
Win32::PerlVersion
Win32::Registry::GetKeys
Win32::Registry::Open
```

## CHAPTER 9

Perl for Web Pages

This chapter covers:

- The common gateway interface (CGI)
- Creating CGI scripts in Perl
- Creating dynamic Web pages from Perl
- Creating Web forms and using Perl to process the data
- Creating a self-maintaining Web page

How Web Pages Work

Even if you've been living in a cave, chances are you haven't missed the Internet phenomenon. This chapter briefly introduces the Web and covers how to use Perl to create dynamic Web pages.

The most popular part of the Internet remains the World Wide Web. With the Web, you run a client program, called a browser, on your system.

The browser, such as Netscape **Navigator** or Microsoft **Internet Explorer**, sends a request to a Web server. The server sends back a response, a Web document. The browser then displays this document for you.

The way the browser determines which server to send the request to is based on the *universal resource locator* (URL), the equivalent of email addresses for Web documents. The URL identifies the type of request, such as `http` (Web), `ftp`, `news`, or `mailto`; the network name of the server machine; and the name of the data requested. In most cases, the requested information is a file or at least a stream of bytes.

The *common gateway interface*, or CGI for short, exists as a gateway between the World Wide Web and other sources of data, such as a database or online catalog.

The Common Gateway Interface

The whole idea of the common gateway interface is that you can extend the concept of a Web page to be a program that just happens to generate a Web page as its output. The Web browser then displays the output of this program, treating the output as an HTML file. Quite a few of these CGI programs are Perl scripts, called CGI scripts in the general usage.

The CGI URL

CGI scripts execute from a URL, the universal resource locator that identifies every Web page. To get the CGI script to execute, the URL must follow the naming conventions established by the Web server (and your site administrator). For example, some sites require CGI scripts to be in a particular directory, usually named **cgi-bin**. Other sites require that CGI scripts have a file extension of *.cgi*. For example, a URL for the following **hello1.cgi** script could be

```
http://www.efjohnson.fun/~erc/cgi-bin/hello1.cgi
```

The preceding host name is not a real system.

N O T E

The rules all depend on how your Web server is configured. You can find out more on this by talking to your Web site administrator.

How CGI Scripts Work

The inside of a CGI script is the same as any other Perl script. The Web server executes this script with the Perl interpreter.

NOTE CGI scripts run on the server machine. Java applets get downloaded from the server and run on the browser machine. This makes CGI scripts great for querying databases or online catalogs or otherwise interacting with large data sets stored on a server. Java applets are better for tasks that run primarily on the user's side of the network.

CGI scripts get data from the Web server one of two ways: the Web server may fill in a large number of environment variables (%ENV in Perl) or may pass data on the command line or both. It's up to your script to deal with this data, extracting it from whatever source is in use.

CGI scripts then send the output HTML data to STDOUT. The Web server intercepts this (probably using a pipe, as discussed in Chapter 6) and passes the data, printed to STDOUT by your script, to the Web browser.

HyperText Markup Language

The HyperText Markup Language, or HTML, is the *lingua franca* of the Web. Web browsers interpret the tags in an HTML document as formatting or linking (hypertext) information. So, if you're creating an interactive Web document, your CGI script must output its data with the proper HTML tags or the user won't see a nicely formatted document—or any document at all. (There are other types of output than HTML, but the vast majority of CGI scripts output HTML-formatted data.)

Using Perl for CGI Scripts

Perl is great for CGI scripts mostly because of its text-handling capability. Since HTML is a text-based format and since the output of any CGI script is an HTML file sent to STDOUT, Perl is one of the best choices for formatting HTML and filling in data into the text stream.

Normally, Perl CGI scripts use the special UNIX comment that identifies **perl** as the program to run to execute the script, such as the following:

```
#!/usr/bin/perl
```

This, of course, works only for UNIX systems. You may also need to use a special suffix, like *.cgi*, for the Web server to accept your script.

Creating a Web Page from a Script

To create a Web page from a script, you must output all the HTML tags yourself. If you've ever created an HTML file from a text editor, you're an old hand at this task. In addition, you must preface the HTML with the MIME Content-type identifier, as shown here:

```
Content-type: text/html
```

The Content-type line must be followed by a blank line.

N O T E

For example, to create a simple Web page from a CGI script, you can use the following:

```
#!/usr/bin/perl
#
# CGI script that outputs a Web page.
#

#
# Note blank line after content type
# is essential.
#
print "Content-type: text/html\n\n";

# HTML header section.

print "<html>\n";
print "<head>\n";
print "<title>Hello From Perl</title>\n";
print "</head>\n";
```

```
# HTML body

print "<body>\n";

# Heading
print "<h1>Yow</h1>\n";

print "Hello, world.\n";

print "<p>\n";        # Paragraph

# End HTML page.
print "</body>\n";
print "</html>\n";

# hello1.cgi
```

This script creates a Web page like the one shown in Figure 9.1.

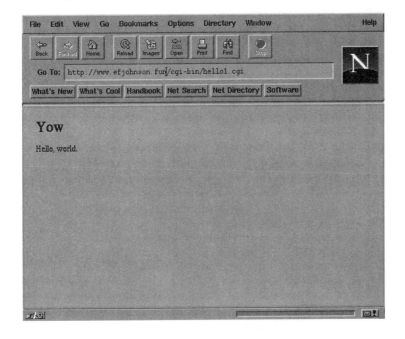

Figure 9.1 A simple Web page from a script.

Launching the Perl Script from Your Web Browser

If you follow the proper conventions for your Web server, the **hello1.cgi** script will get executed if you try to call up this file as a URL.

Security and CGI Scripts

Some sites simply don't allow CGI scripts from end users, due to security concerns (legitimate concerns, by the way). Other sites require all CGI scripts reside in a special directory. You'll need to resolve these issues with your system administrator.

Using the CGI Module

While there are many CGI-related Perl modules to help you create CGI scripts, the **CGI.pm** module provides one of the simplest introductions to CGI scripts and forms. New with Perl 5, **CGI.pm** replaces the **un-cgi.pl** and **cgi-lib.pl** that were common with Perl 4.

Look in the **contrib/www** directory for the **CGI.pm** module as well as other CGI- and Web-related modules.

CD-ROM

To show how the CGI module works, we can revisit the simple Web page created in the preceding **hello1.cgi** script. This script built up a Web page manually, using the Perl print command to output every piece of HTML required for a Web page.

With the CGI module, you can take advantage of built-in subroutines to output most of the more tedious aspects of HTML. You'll still call print for a lot of the content of your Web page, but you'll be able to avoid the title area and so on, by using the handy header, start_html and end_html subroutines in the CGI module.

The following **hello2.cgi** script provides a hello world Web page using the more convenient CGI module:

```
#!/usr/bin/perl
#
# CGI script using CGI.pm module.
#
use CGI;

$page = new CGI;

# Print page header.
print $page->header;

print $page->start_html(
    -title=>'Hello from perl',
    -BGCOLOR=>'white');

# HTML body

# Heading
print "<h1>Hello</h1>\n";

print "Hello, from perl and the CGI module.";
print "<p>\n";  # Paragraph

# End HTML page.
print $page->end_html;

# hello2.cgi
```

The -title=>'Hello from perl' syntax in the preceding **hello2.cgi** script is another new form of specifying parameters to a subroutine. The => really just replaces the comma. You can use the => syntax to name the parameter to set and the value. For example, the following calls to a subroutine are equivalent:

```
$page->start_html('Hello from perl',
    'white');

$page->start_html(-title=>'Hello from perl',
    -BGCOLOR=>'white');
```

The new syntax just lets you name a parameter. You can also skip the parameter name and use => in place of a comma.

The Web page created by the **hello2.cgi** script appears in Figure 9.2.

Figure 9.2 The second hello Web page.

While written for UNIX, the **CGI.pm** script works on Windows as well, but you must make a few changes. First, in the **CGI.pm** file, modify the line that states:

WINDOWS

```
$OS='UNIX';
```

Change this to

```
$OS='WINDOWS';
```

In addition, to get CGI scripts to work, you need to place them in special locations, depending on your Web server software. See your server documentation for more on this. **CGI.pm** should work with EMWACS, IIS, Purveyor, and WebSite.

Testing the Script

Another nice part of the CGI module is that you can test the script from the command line, before you hook it up to a Web server. Just run your script. The CGI module will ask for any input, which you can end by entering **Control-D** (the UNIX end-of-file marker). The input you would provide are the names of input fields and their values (see the following section on data-entry forms). Then, you'll see the **hello2.cgi** script output HTML, as shown next:

```
(offline mode: enter name=value pairs on standard input)
Content-type: text/html

<HTML><HEAD><TITLE>Hello from perl</TITLE>
</HEAD><BODY BGCOLOR="white"><h1>Hello</h1>
Hello, from perl and the CGI module.<p>
```

This off-line mode helps you test your scripts.

While you can use Perl to create Web pages automatically, the more interesting uses come when you add user interaction and let users fill in values in data-entry forms.

Data-Entry Forms in Web Pages

Most Web browsers support some form of data entry. The user fills in data and then presses a **Submit** button to send the data to a program—a CGI script. The CGI script then extracts the data from the browser, processes the data, for example, looks up a record in a database, and outputs a HTML Web page as a result.

We've already covered creating Web pages Perl. The next step is making a fill-in-the-blanks form and then processing that form.

Web Forms

All HTML is based on the idea of tags, and so are HTML forms. To create a data-entry form, you need to use the `<FORM>` tag, as shown in the following **form1.htm** Web document:

```
<html>
<head>
<title>Form #1</title>
</head>

<body>

<FORM METHOD="POST"
 ACTION="http://www.efjohnson.fun/~erc/cgi-bin/form1.cgi">

<H2>Customer Order Tracking</H2>

Enter order number:
<INPUT NAME="orderno">
<p>

<INPUT TYPE="submit" VALUE="Look up">

</FORM>

</body>
</html>
```

 See Appendix A for a list of HTML references. If this HTML stuff really blows you away, for now just use the Web pages as provided. You can later look up more information on HTML. You'll find such knowledge very helpful for your career.

The <FORM> tag, which specifies the method used to send data to your script, uses the POST method (the default). The ACTION part specifies the URL of the CGI script to execute for the form. You need to use the <FORM> tag to bracket all your data-entry tags. (You can use multiple <FORM> tags on one page, but such usage is beyond the scope of this book. See Appendix A for a listing of HTML books.)

The <INPUT> tag forms the simplest data-entry field. By default, an <INPUT> tag creates a text-entry area. You must provide a name (*orderno* in this case). You'll use the name in your Perl script to look up the value the user typed into the data-entry field. You also use <INPUT> tags for the

Submit button. The user presses this button when all the data are entered and the user wants to submit the data to the Web server.

The data gets sent to the `ACTION` URL listed in the `<FORM>` tag. Web forms follow the model that the user enters data and only when complete does the Web server send the data to your CGI script. The **Submit** button does just that.

When you display this page in a Web browser, you'll see something like Figure 9.3.

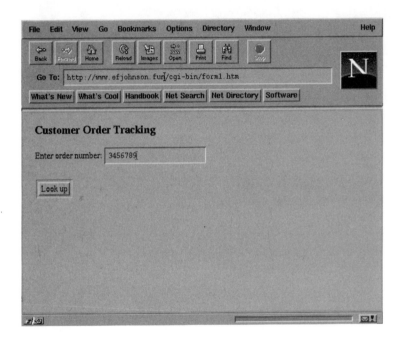

Figure 9.3 A data-entry form.

A Perl Script to Process a Form

The Perl script to process this form follows:

```
#!/usr/bin/perl
#
# CGI script using CGI.pm module.
```

```perl
#
use CGI;

$form = new CGI;

#
# Extract value of order number.
# The name must match the name in
# the Web page for this INPUT field.
#
$orderno = $form->param('orderno');

# Print form header.
print $form->header;

print $form->start_html(
    -title=>'Customer Order Tracking',
    -BGCOLOR=>'white');

# HTML body

# Heading
print "<h1>Your Order Number</h1>\n";

print "Your order number was: $orderno.\n";
print "<p>\n";   # Paragraph

# End HTML form.
print $form->end_html;

# form1.cgi
```

As you can see, the **form1.cgi** script creates a new HTML Web page and prints the page information, just as the **hello2.cgi** script did before. The use of the param subroutine to query the value of the named data-entry field is new in this script.

You must use the name of the data-entry item in the Web form, orderno in this case. The param subroutine retrieves the value the user typed into this field and returns the data, which gets placed into the $orderno variable. (You can use any variable you want.)

The Web page output by the **form1.cgi** script appears in Figure 9.4.

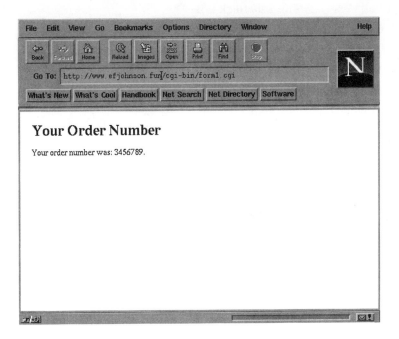

Figure 9.4 Output from the Web form.

More Data-Entry Options

In addition to the default <INPUT> text-entry field, you can create a number of other data-entry widgets with the <INPUT> tag. For the <INPUT> tag, you can use any of the types listed in Table 9.1.

223

Table 9.1 Types for the <INPUT> tag.

Type	Usage
"text"	Text-entry field, the default.
"password"	Text-entry field with obscured input.
"checkbox"	An on-off check box.
"radio"	An on-off check box, of which only one of the radio buttons with the same name can be on.
"submit"	Special button to send data to Web server.
"reset"	Special button to reset form to original values.

You can use these extended types in a Web page like the one shown in Figure 9.5.

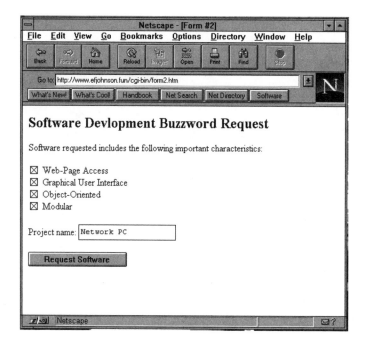

Figure 9.5 Adding more types of input.

The HTML for the page in Figure 9.5 follows:

```
<html>
<head>
<title>Form #2</title>
</head>

<body>

<FORM METHOD="POST"
 ACTION="http://www.efjohnson.fun/~erc/cgi-bin/form2.cgi">

<H2>Software Development Buzzword Request</H2>

Software requested includes the following important
characteristics:
<p>

<INPUT NAME="web" TYPE="checkbox" VALUE="yes">
Web-Page Access
<br>

<INPUT NAME="gui" TYPE="checkbox" VALUE="yes">
Graphical User Interface
<br>

<INPUT NAME="oop" TYPE="checkbox" VALUE="yes">
Object-Oriented
<br>

<INPUT NAME="mod" TYPE="checkbox" VALUE="yes">
Modular
<p>

Project name:
<INPUT NAME="projectname">
<p>
```

```
<INPUT TYPE="submit" VALUE="Request Software">

</FORM>

</body>
</html>
```

When the user submits the request, for new software development, the **form2.cgi** script responds with a Web page as shown in Figure 9.6.

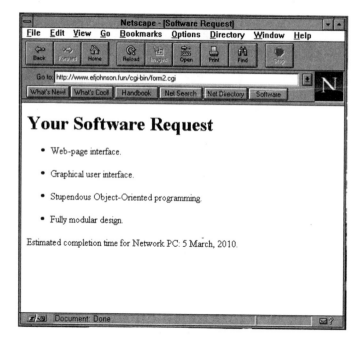

Figure 9.6 When you'll see the software you requested.

The script to process this data follows:

```
#!/usr/bin/perl
#
# CGI script for form2.htm.
#
use CGI;
```

```perl
$form = new CGI;

#
# Extract value of buzzwords.
#
$web = $form->param('web');
$gui = $form->param('gui');
$oop = $form->param('oop');
$mod = $form->param('mod');
$proj = $form->param('projectname');

# Print form header.
print $form->header;

print $form->start_html(
    -title=>'Software Request',
    -BGCOLOR=>'white');

# HTML body

# Heading
print "<h1>Your Software Request</h1>\n";
print "<UL>\n";
if ($web eq "yes") {
    print "<LI>Web-page interface.<p>\n";
}

if ($gui eq "yes") {
    print "<LI>Graphical user interface.<p>\n";
}

if ($oop eq "yes") {
    print "<LI>Stupendous Object-Oriented programming.<p>\n";
}

if ($mod eq "yes") {
    print "<LI>Fully modular design.<p>\n";
}
print "</UL>\n";

print "Estimated completion time for $proj: 5 March, 2010.";
```

```
print "<p>\n";  # Paragraph

# End HTML form.
print $form->end_html;

# form2.cgi
```

Scrolled Lists and Option Menus

In addition to the <INPUT> tag, you can use the <SELECT> tag to display a scrolled list or option menu. For <SELECT>, you must use the <SELECT>...</SELECT> format. Between the tags, you place <OPTION> tags, which specify the data to display for an option the user can pick.

The <SELECT> tag must have a name. You can also specify a size, which is then used to control the display. If the size is 2 or more, the options will appear in a scrolled list. If the size is 1 (or missing), an option menu appears.

Figure 9.7 shows both type of widgets.

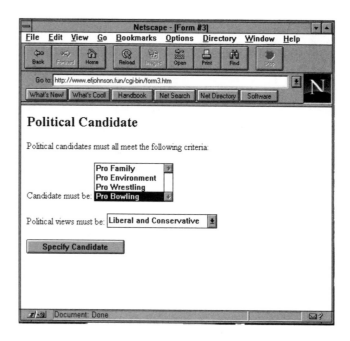

Figure 9.7 Using <SELECT> tags in a form.

The HTML file for this form follows:

```
<html>
<head>
<title>Form #3</title>
</head>

<body>

<FORM METHOD="POST"
 ACTION="http://www.efjohnson.fun/erc/cgi-bin/form3.cgi">

<H2>Political Candidate</H2>

Political candidates must all meet
the following criteria:
<p>

Candidate must be:
<SELECT NAME="pro" SIZE=4>
<OPTION>Pro Family
<OPTION>Pro Environment
<OPTION>Pro Wrestling
<OPTION>Pro Bowling
</SELECT>
<p>

Political views must be:
<SELECT NAME="wing" SIZE=1>
<OPTION>Liberal and Conservative
<OPTION>Conservative and Liberal
</SELECT>
<p>

<INPUT TYPE="submit" VALUE="Specify Candidate">
<p>
</FORM>
```

```
</body>
</html>
```

In your CGI script, the value for each of the <SELECT> tags will be the text of the <OPTION> selected. If nothing was selected in a scrolled list, your script gets nothing.

The script to process this form follows:

```
#!/usr/bin/perl
#
# CGI script for form3.htm.
#
use CGI;

$form = new CGI;

#
# Extract value of buzzwords.
#
$favor = $form->param('pro');
$wing = $form->param('wing');

# Print form header.
print $form->header;

print $form->start_html(
    -title=>'Political Candidate',
    -BGCOLOR=>'white');

# HTML body

# Heading
print "<h1>Your Candidate</h1>\n";

if ($favor eq "") {
    print "Is in favor of: nothing<p>\n";
} else {
    print "Is in favor of: $favor<p>\n";
}
```

```
print "and leans to the $wing views.<p>\n";

# End HTML form.
print $form->end_html;

# form3.cgi
```

Entering More Text

The `<TEXTAREA>` tag provides for multiline text input. Other than that, it acts pretty much like an `<INPUT>` tag. Table 9.2 lists the attributes for the `<TEXTAREA>` tag.

Table 9.2 Attributes for the `<TEXTAREA>` tag.

Attribute	Controls
NAME	(Mandatory) Name used in Perl script to extract data.
ROWS	Number of visible rows of text.
COLS	Number of visible columns of text.

NOTE For the columns, the size of the user's font and browser window controls how much the user can see. While you can't control this size, I've found a value of 60 columns works well on most browsers.

Adding a Reset Button

An `<INPUT>` tag with a TYPE of `"reset"` creates a button that will reset all fields in the form to the original values. You can create such a button in the Web page with the following HTML:

```
<INPUT TYPE="reset" VALUE="Reset Form">
```

We can put this together and create a form to enter in a number of rows of text, as shown in Figure 9.8.

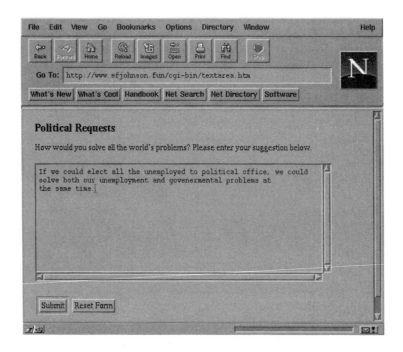

Figure 9.8 Entering multiple rows of text.

The HTML source for this Web page follows:

```
<html>
<head>
<title>TEXTAREA</title>
</head>

<body>

<FORM METHOD="POST"
 ACTION="http://www.efjohnson.fun/erc/cgi-bin/textarea.cgi">

<H2>Political Requests</H2>

How would you solve all the world's problems?
Please enter your suggestion below.
<p>
```

```
<TEXTAREA NAME="suggestion" ROWS=12 COLS=60>
Default data goes here.
</TEXTAREA>
<p>
```

```
<INPUT TYPE="submit" VALUE="Submit">
<INPUT TYPE="reset" VALUE="Reset Form">

</FORM>

</body>
</html>
```

The Perl CGI script that processes this form creates a new Web page, as shown in Figure 9.9.

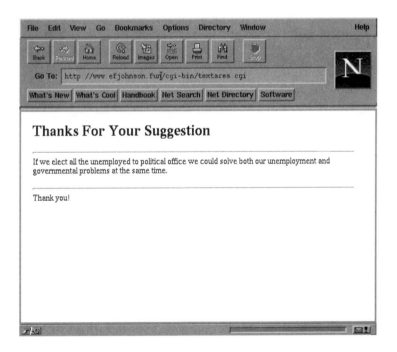

Figure 9.9 Responding to the user's suggestion.

The script that created this page follows:

```perl
#!/usr/bin/perl
#
# CGI script for textarea.htm.
#
use CGI;

$form = new CGI;

#
# Extract value of buzzwords.
#
@suggest = $form->param('suggestion');

# Print form header.
print $form->header;

print $form->start_html(
    -title=>'Thanks',
    -BGCOLOR=>'white');

# HTML body

# Heading
print "<h1>Thanks For Your Suggestion</h1>\n";

print "<hr>";    # Horizontal rule
print "@suggest\n";
print "<p>\n";   # Paragraph
print "<hr>";    # Horizontal rule

print "Thank you!";
print "<p>\n";   # Paragraph

# End HTML form.
print $form->end_html;

# textarea.cgi
```

Passing Data On the Command Line

Many online databases allow you to enter a query directly from a hypertext link, rather than force you to fill out a form. The way this works is that the link encodes the data for the query in the URL. For example, the following URL really calls a CGI script and passes query information as command-line parameters:

```
http://www.efjohnson.fun/cgi-bin/cmdline.cgi?p1+p2+p3+p4
```

The Web server decodes all the data after the question mark, ?, as command-line parameters. The plus characters, +, replace spaces in the URL.

In the preceding example, the CGI script, **cmdline.cgi**, gets called with the following parameters in @ARGV:

```
p1 p2 p3 p4
```

You can take advantage of this with a script like the following:

```perl
#!/usr/bin/perl
#
# CGI script for form3.htm.
#
use CGI;

$form = new CGI;

print $form->header;

print $form->start_html(
    -title=>'8-Ball',
    -BGCOLOR=>'white');

print "<h1>Your Answer</h1>\n";

print "Your query was: @ARGV<p>\n";
```

```
print "Sorry, ask again later.<p>\n";

# End HTML form.
print $form->end_html;

# cmdline.cgi
```

Instead of a form, the HTML file just displays a hypertext link, as shown here:

```
<html>
<head>
<title>Command-Line CGI</title>
</head>

<body>
<H2>Online Query System</H2>

Ask the
<A HREF="http://www.efjohnson.fun/erc/cgi-bin/cmdline.cgi?p1+p2+p3+p4">
Internet Eight-Ball</A> to answer your questions.

</body>
</html>
```

NOTE This type of CGI script is often called an <ISINDEX> query.

The Self-Maintaining Web Page

As anyone who's ever created a Web page will attest to, Web pages are a pain to keep up to date. Just about as soon as you've finished your page, new data arrive or old data become obsolete, and you need to update your page. All of a sudden, your once useful Web page slips into disuse as it becomes out of date. Perl can help in creating the elusive self-maintaining Web page. Of course, Perl can't do everything, but it can certainly help maintain your Web information.

One of the problems in maintaining a Web page is indexing the material. Most of my Web pages present a number of topics, such as troubleshooting tips for the GroupWise email or ClearCase configuration management software, or frequently asked questions regarding running **Tcl** scripts on Windows. The information appears as a lot of related topics, for which I must maintain a table of contents and update all the links. The main problem is lack of time. It takes time to add a new topic manually to the document and insert the new table of contents information.

So, since Perl provides strong text-handling capabilities, one way to help ease the burden is to generate the Web page automatically. If you store each topic as a separate file, then you can use Perl to create the HTML page from all the topics. Perl can also generate the table of contents section at the top of the page, from the list of all topics used to generate the file. The CGI module can help in outputting the HTML structure.

Another major problem is updating the data. Users of Web pages often submit new tips via email. The problem is then inserting the new tip into the Web page. Perl, and the CGI module, can help with this, too. At the end of your Web page, you can create a data-entry form to allow any user to add a new topic—all automatically—thus creating the self-maintaining Web page. Users fill in forms, which creates new topics, and Perl automates creating a new page from all the topics.

Of course, it isn't as easy as it sounds. For one thing, you probably want to examine all the input, especially if your page is accessible from the Internet. I'll leave that part up to you. (Remember that users might add HTML tags to the topics they provide, and with modern browsers, HTML tags can control the downloading of applets or other program execution.)

The next sections describe how you can automate many of the tasks for maintaining a Web page. The beginning sections discuss the theory, and the later sections show the HTML pages and CGI scripts to implement the theory. How much you choose to automate is up to you, but you'll find that you can automate away a lot of the pain of maintaining Web pages. Even if you're not planning to create a self-maintaining page, the following sections make extensive use of Perl for CGI and HTML, providing examples of how you can put your Web pages together using Perl.

Building a Web Page from Major Sections

If each topic is stored in a separate file, you can use Perl's file commands to read in each file and concatenate the files, adding dribbles of HTML tags to make the page look better, such as HTML heading tags around the title of each section. Of course, we'd like things sorted a little better than just concatenating files together, as well as an automatically generated table of contents. To do this, you can take advantage of the fact that you can store a lot of data into a Perl variable, adding text and text to a scalar variable.

Adding Topics within Each Section

One style of organization that works for me is to divide the Web page into major sections and topics. A major section could be a general theme, like problems printing. A topic within that section could be tips for working with a Hewlett-Packard laser printer. I've generally found this sort of hierarchy works well for technical documents.

To manage the idea of sections and topics within a section, you can use Perl's associative arrays. One array, @sections, holds the name of each section.

This second array holds the text of each topic within a section. This array, %topics, is an associative array. The keys in this associative array are the topic names, prefaced with the section name to make them unique (so more than one section can have a topic named "Common Problems," for example). The values in the %topics associative array are the actual text of the topic, as many lines as necessary, all stuffed into one scalar value. This is just one way to implement this scheme; I'm sure you can come up with zillions of other ways.

The sections can be separated by HTML lines, using the <HR> (horizontal rule—or line) tag. This is easy to generate with the print command.

Generating a Table of Contents from the Topics

Once you have a set of topics, you'd like to see a table of contents, particularly for large documents. In HTML, you can have each entry in the table of contents link to start of the topic, using local jumps in HTML.

Using an HTML definition list, with the <DL> tag, you can tag each section name with a <DT> and each topic underneath the section with a <DD>. This will output a table of contents as shown in Figure 9.10.

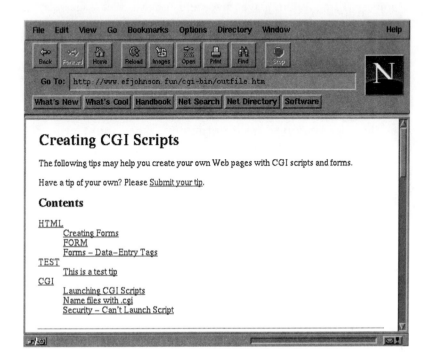

Figure 9.10 A table of contents.

Allowing the User to Add Topics

To allow users to add new topics, all you need is a data-entry form. The Perl CGI script that processes the form needs to save the data to a file on disk. Another script, the following **regen.pl** script, recreates the Web page from all the files, including the new files. The reason for separating the scripts is security.

WARNING

Be very careful with allowing the user to create disk files. For that reason, the user won't see the new topic right away. Instead, you must go in and recreate the Web page yourself, by running the **regen.pl** script. I'm doing this to force you to examine the contents of the new topics. Because the topics will appear in a Web page and because Web pages can execute scripts and Java applets, you have to be very careful. While this detracts from the automation, it's better to be safe than sorry.

Responding to the User's Input

Whenever the user provides any information, you should provide some form of feedback, especially since the user was nice enough to provide information for *your* page. Figure 9.11 shows one type of feedback page.

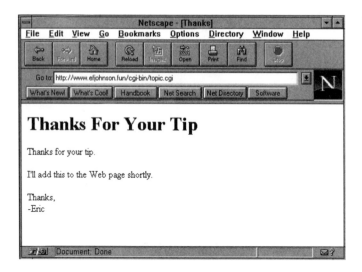

Figure 9.11 A thank-you page.

The HTML for this page follows:

```
<html>
<head>
<title>Thanks</title>
```

```
</head>

<body>
<H2>Thanks</H2>

Thanks for your tip.
<p>
I'll add this to the Web page shortly.
<p>
Thanks,
<br>
-Eric
<p>

</body>
</html>
```

You can either keep this thank-you page in a separate file, and load it in at run time, or use Perl commands to output the page.

Handling Bad Input

Whenever the user can enter values, there's always the chance for bad input. If this happens, your CGI scripts will need to be able to display an HTML page that describes the problem. One way of dealing with errors is to announce them to the user with a cryptic error message. (*No keyboard found; press F1 to continue* and *Pre-Newtonian degeneracy discovered* have always been my favorite error messages.)

To make a more robust system, you may want to fix the errors silently. For example, if the user tries to enter data for a topic that already exists, why not just extend that topic with the new text? (Or, simply ignore the fact that the topic names are the same and add a new topic reusing the same topic name.) If the section can't be found, then create a new section. This leaves few errors.

Creating New Topics

When the user enters in a new topic, a file gets stored to disk; the script chooses a unique file name. Once the file gets stored, it's time to regenerate the Web page. But, due to security concerns, the page doesn't get updated right away. It's up to you to run the **regen.pl** script to regenerate the Web page with the new topic. To pull this all together, the CGI script that handles user entry of new topics follows:

```perl
#!/usr/bin/perl
#
# CGI script for topic.htm.
#
use CGI;

$form = new CGI;

#
# Extract the data.
#
$section = $form->param('section');
$topic   = $form->param('topic');
$user    = $form->param('user');
@suggest = $form->param('suggestion');

#
# Now, save the data to disk. To do so,
# choose a unique file name.
#
$filename = &Get_filename();

open(OUTPUT, ">$filename") or
    die "Can't open $filename";

print OUTPUT "$section\n";
print OUTPUT "$topic\n";
print OUTPUT "$user\n";
print OUTPUT "@suggest\n";

close(OUTPUT);

# Print response.
```

```perl
print $form->header;

print $form->start_html(
    -title=>'Thanks',
    -BGCOLOR=>'white');

# HTML body

# Heading
print "<h1>Thanks For Your Tip</h1>\n";

print "Thanks for your tip.<p>\n";
print "I'll add this to the Web page shortly.<p>\n";
print "Thanks,<br>\n";
print "-Eric<p>\n";

# End HTML form.
print $form->end_html;

#
# Uses a brute-force method to determine a
# unique file name.
#

sub Get_filename {
    my($found) = 0;
    my($filename);
    my($letter) = 65;    # "A"
    my($i) = 0;

    #
    # Search for a file name.
    #
    while ( ! $found ) {

        $filename = chr($letter) . $i . ".top";

        #
```

```
# Check if file exists.
#
if ( -e $filename ) {
    $i++;

    if ($i > 9999) {
        $i = 0;
        $letter++;
    }

    #
    # Sanity check.
    # If we have too many files,
    # overwrite last.
    #
    if ($letter > 92) {
        return $filename;
    }
} else {
    $found = 1;    # Done.
}
}

    return $filename;
}

# topic.cgi
```

The **topic.cgi** script extracts the section heading, topic title, user name and suggestion from the **topic.htm** Web form. Then, the script finds a unique file on disk (using a method that could easily be improved), storing the data to that file. The file names chosen will include **A0.top, A1.top, A999.top, B0.top,** and so on. The *.top* extension has no meaning other than it's short for *topic*.

The whole idea is to store each topic in a separate file. The following **regen.pl** script then combines all the separate topics into one HTML file for the user to see.

Generating a Thank-You List

Since users are so nice as to provide information for your Web page, you might as well publicly thank them with a special thank-you section at the end of the page. This is rather easy to generate if you have a section for users to enter their name in the form. Some users may want to leave this field blank, of course.

Putting It All Together: The Self-Maintaining Web Page

Pulling all these separate topics together, you get a data-entry form like the one shown in Figure 9.12.

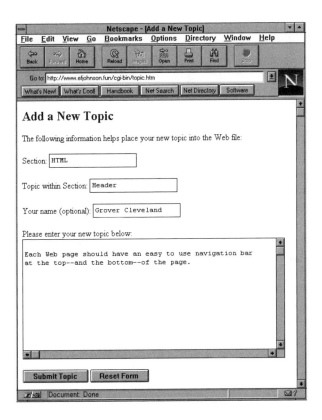

Figure 9.12 The self-maintaining Web page.

245

The HTML for this form follows:

```
<html>
<head>
<title>Add a New Topic</title>
</head>

<body>

<FORM METHOD="POST"
 ACTION="http://www.efjohnson.fun/~erc/cgi-bin/topic.cgi">

<H2>Add a New Topic</H2>

The following information helps place your new topic
into the Web file:
<p>
Section:
<INPUT NAME="section">
<p>
Topic within Section:
<INPUT NAME="topic">
<p>
Your name (optional):
<INPUT NAME="user">
<p>

Please enter your new topic below:
<TEXTAREA NAME="suggestion" ROWS=12 COLS=60>

</TEXTAREA>
<p>

<INPUT TYPE="submit" VALUE="Submit Topic">
<INPUT TYPE="reset" VALUE="Reset Form">

</FORM>
```

```
</body>
</html>
```

This form is a separate page. You could just as easily place the form into the main Web page that gets created by the **regen.pl** script. One way to handle any extra data you might want to place in the Web page is the concept of a header and a footer. Both the header and footer are simply HTML documents (or, more likely, partial HTML documents). The header gets included before any of the automatically generated HTML data. The footer gets added to the end of the document.

In this case, both the header and the footer contain links to the **topic.htm** form shown previously. The **footer.htm** follows:

```
Have a tip of your own? Please
<A HREF="topic.htm">Submit your tip</A>.
<p>

</body>
</html>
```

Both the footer and the header exist to allow you to place any HTML elements you'd like into the Web page. For example, you may want a company logo or a navigation bar.

The header used for this simple page follows:

```
<html>
<head>
<title>Creating CGI Scripts</title>
</head>

<body BGCOLOR='white'>

<H1>Creating CGI Scripts</H1>

The following tips may help you create
your own Web pages with CGI scripts
and forms.
<p>
```

```
Have a tip of your own? Please
<A HREF="topic.htm">Submit your tip</A>.
<p>
```

248

Both the header and the footer link to the **topic.htm** page that allows the user to add a new topic. You could also place that page directly in the footer, if you desire.

The rest of the page is automatically generated from the header file, the footer file, and all the topic files.

Regenerating the Web Page

One large Perl script, **regen.pl**, regenerates the entire Web page. To do this, it needs to pull together data from a number of sources, including

- A header HTML file, shown previously, to allow you to place a consistent header and navigation links for all your Web pages.
- An HTML footer file, also to allow navigation links.
- All the topic files created by you or by users.
- A link to the update form, shown in Figure 9.12.

The output Web page follows a similar format:

1. The contents of the header file.
2. The table of contents, generated from all the topic names.
3. The topics themselves.
4. The thank-you section, naming all the people who have contributed.
5. The date the form was created.
6. The contents of the footer file.

It's the job of the **regen.pl** script to pull all this together and create an output Web page. Because this script is run at a later time, it does not need to follow the conventions of CGI scripts; this script is not executed by the Web server.

Instead, you call **regen.pl** from the command line, with all the necessary files. This script seems a bit complicated, but really uses only basic Perl constructs introduced in earlier chapters. In fact, I'm sure you can come up with more efficient methods to perform some of the tasks.

The **regen.pl** script follows:

```
#
# Creates a Web page from a series of topics.
#
# Usage:
#    perl regen.pl outfile.htm header.htm footer.htm *.top
#

# Open all files for error-checking.

if ($#ARGV < 3) {
    print "ERROR: Usage is:\n";
    print "perl regen.pl outfile.htm ";
    print "header.htm footer.htm \*.top\n";

    exit;
}

open (OUTFILE, ">$ARGV[0]" ) or
  die "Can't open output file $ARGV[0]";

open (HEADER, $ARGV[1] ) or
  die "Can't open header file $ARGV[1]";

open (FOOTER, $ARGV[2] ) or
  die "Can't open footer file $ARGV[2]";

# Make outfile the default output.
select(OUTFILE);

# Process all topic files.
$i = 3;
while ( $i <= $#ARGV ) {
```

```perl
        print STDERR "Reading file \"$ARGV[$i]\"\n";

        &Read_topic_file( $ARGV[$i] );

        $i++;
}

#
# Now that all the data are read in,
# generate the output.
#

# Process header.
&Header;

#
# Generate a table of contents from all topics.
#
&Generate_contents;

# Process sections and topic output.
&Output_sections;

#
# Output a thank-you list.
#
&Thank_you;

#
# Output a date-stamp.
#
&Date_stamp;

#
# Process footer; this file should contain
# the data-entry form as well as any stylistic
# conventions for your site.
#
```

```perl
&Footer;

# Close all files
close(HEADER);
close(FOOTER);
close(OUTFILE);

#
# Reads in a topic file.
#
# Usage:
#     &Read_topic_file("filename");
#
sub Read_topic_file {

    my($filename) = $_[0];
    my($sectionname);
    my($topicname);
    my($username);
    my($fullname);
    my($data);

    open (TOPIC, $filename) or
        die "Can't open topic file $filename";

    # Topic and section name are first two lines.
    $sectionname = <TOPIC>;
    chomp($sectionname);

    $topicname = <TOPIC>;
    chomp($topicname);

    # Third line is user name or blank.
    $username = <TOPIC>;
    chomp($username);
    &Add_username($username);

    # Add data to topic list.
```

```perl
$fullname = $sectionname . "/" . $topicname;

# Read in rest of file.
$topics{$fullname} = "";

$data = <TOPIC>;

while ($data) {

    chomp($data);

    if ($data eq "") {
        # Add paragraph markers.
        $topics{$fullname} =
            $topics{$fullname} . "<p>\n";
    } else {
        $topics{$fullname} =
            $topics{$fullname} . $data . "\n";
    }

    $data = <TOPIC>;
}

close($filename);

# Add section, if new.
&Add_section($sectionname);
}

#
# Adds a section to the list of
# sections, if new.
#
# Usage:
#    &Add_section("sectionname");
#
sub Add_section {
    my($sectionname) = $_[0];
```

```perl
    my($element);
    my(@section_list) = @sections;

    #
    # Check if section name is
    # already present. See
    # if you can find more
    # efficient ways to check.
    #
    foreach $element (@section_list) {

        if ($element eq $sectionname) {
            return;
        }
    }

    # If no match, add item to list.
    unshift(@sections, $sectionname);
}

#
# Adds user name to list; may be blank.
#
# Usage:
#    &Add_username($username);
#
sub Add_username {
    my($user) = $_[0];
    my($element);
    my(@user_list) = @userlist;

    #
    # Check if user name is
    # already present. See
    # if you can find more
    # efficient ways to check.
    #
    foreach $element (@user_list) {
```

```perl
            if ($element eq $user) {
                return;
            }
        }

        # If no match, add item to list.
        unshift(@userlist, $user);

}


#
# Reads in header file and outputs it.
# Assumes:
#     a) Header file handle HEADER is opened.
#     b) Header file has valid HTML.
#
# Usage:
#     &Header;
#
sub Header {
    my(@data) = <HEADER>;

    print "@data\n";
}


#
# Reads in footer file and outputs it.
# Assumes:
#     a) Footer file handle FOOTER is opened.
#     b) Footer file has valid HTML.
#
# Usage:
#     &Footer;
#
sub Footer {
    my(@data) = <FOOTER>;

    print "@data\n";
```

```perl
}

#
# Generates a table of contents
# as a <DL> list.
#
sub Generate_contents {

    my($sect);
    my($shortname);
    my($topicname);
    my(@sorted);
    my(@topic_list);

    print "<H2>Contents</H2>\n";

    # Use a definition list for Contents.
    print "<DL>\n";
    foreach $sect (@sections) {
        # For each section, a DT tag.
        print "<DT><A HREF=\"\#$sect\">$sect</A>\n";

        # For each topic in a section,
        # a DD tag. All topic names start
        # with the section name.
        @topic_list = keys(%topics);

        @sorted = sort(@topic_list);

        foreach $topicname (@sorted) {

            if ($topicname =~ /^$sect/) {
                $shortname =
                    &Get_topic_name($topicname);

                print "<DD><A HREF=\"\#$topicname\">";
                print "$shortname</A>\n";
            }
```

```perl
            }

        }
        print "</DL><p>\n";

    }


    #
    # Outputs all the sections.
    #
    sub Output_sections {
        my($sect);

        foreach $sect (@sections) {
            # Separate sections with a line.
            print "<p><hr><p>\n";

            # Anchor hypertext link.
            print "<H2><A NAME=\"$sect\">$sect</A></H2>\n";

            # Output topics.
            &Output_topics($sect);
        }

    }


    #
    # Outputs all the topics of a section.
    #
    # Usage:
    #    &Output_topics("sectionname");
    #
    sub Output_topics {
        my($sectionname) = $_[0];

        my(@topic_list);
        my(@sorted);
        my($topicname);
```

```perl
    my($shortname);

    # All topic names start with
    # the section name.
    @topic_list = keys(%topics);

    @sorted = sort(@topic_list);

    foreach $topicname (@sorted) {

        # Check if topic is part of section
        if ($topicname =~ /^$sectionname/ ) {

            $shortname =
                &Get_topic_name($topicname);

            # Print topic header and
            # hypertext anchor.
            print "<b><A NAME=\"$topicname\">";
            print "$shortname</A></b><p>\n";

            # Print topic data.
            print "$topics{$topicname}<p>\n";
        }
    }
}


#
# Returns topic name from the
# Section:Topic passed in.
#
# Usage:
#    &Get_topic_name($fullname);
#
sub Get_topic_name {
    my($topicname) = $_[0];
    my($pos);
    my($shortname);
```

```perl
    $pos = index($topicname, "/") + 1;

    $shortname = substr($topicname, $pos);

    return $shortname;
}


#
# Outputs thank-yous.
#
sub Thank_you {

    my($user);

    if (@userlist) {
        print "<p><hr><p>\n";
        print "<b>Thanks to the following:</b><p>\n";
    }

    foreach $user (@userlist) {
        print "$user<br>\n";
    }

    print "<p>\n";
}


#
# Outputs a date-stamp.
#
sub Date_stamp {

    $t = time();

    ($sec, $min, $hour, $dom, $mon,
     $year,$wday, $yday, $isdst) =
       localtime($t);

    $year += 1900;
```

```
# Provide English equivalents.
@months = ("January", "February",
        "March", "April", "May",
        "June", "July", "August",
        "September", "October",
        "November", "December");

    print "Output on $dom $months[$mon], $year.\n";
    print "<p><hr><p>\n";
}

# regen.pl
```

To execute this script, you need to pass the name of the output file, the header file, the footer file, and all the topic file names:

```
perl regen.pl outfile.htm header.htm footer.htm *.top
```

There's a lot more you can do with Perl for working with Web pages. See the libwww, HTTPD, and CGI modules on the CD-ROM for more neat ideas and the Perl subroutines to implement them.

 Look in the **contrib/www** directory.

CD-ROM

Summary

The whole idea of the common gateway interface is that you can extend the concept of a Web page to be a program that just happens to generate a Web page as its output. The Web browser then displays the output of this program, treating the output as an HTML file. The vast majority of these CGI programs are Perl scripts.

The HyperText Markup Language is the *lingua franca* of the Web. Web browsers interpret the tags in an HTML document as formatting or linking (hypertext) information. So, if you're creating an interactive Web document, your CGI script must output its data with the proper HTML tags.

While there are many CGI-related Perl modules to help you create CGI scripts, the **CGI.pm** module provides one of the simplest introductions to CGI scripts and forms.

All HTML is based on the idea of tags and so are HTML forms. To create a data-entry form, you need to use the <FORM> tag. The <INPUT> tag forms the simplest data-entry field. The <SELECT> tag displays a scrolled list or option menu. And the <TEXTAREA> tag provides for multiline text input.

In Chapter 10, you'll see how Perl can be used for cross-platform application development.

Perl Commands Introduced in This Chapter

```
CGI::end_html
CGI::header
CGI::param
CGI::start_html
```

Perl for Cross-Platform Development

This chapter covers:

- Building your software with help from Perl
- Sending email when the build task completes
- Automating rebuilding when the code changes
- Perl in your software environment
- Automated testing
- Scanning for include files
- Generating documentation with Perl
- Generating code with Perl

Automating the Software Development Process

Many software development tasks can be automated. Everyone who uses **make** knows that. Perl fits into the equation because it runs on many platforms and doesn't have the idiosyncratic problems that you get with different versions of **make**, especially **nmake** on Windows.

Because each site tends to use a different software-development process and because of the plethora of computer languages in use, much of this chapter is, by necessity, theoretical. Even so, you'll be surprised at how many areas Perl can help. Areas where Perl can be most effective for automating your software development include checking source code in and out, testing scripts, and starting the build where needed. The main areas fall into two general categories: building your software with help from Perl and using Perl in your software development environment.

Building Your Software with Help from Perl

If you work on any large application or suite of applications, chances are you have a set of scripts to help automate some of the mundane tasks of building and maintaining this software. In addition, these scripts may also provide some uniformity in the software-development process, such as ensuring that all software checked into a master directory has a test script attached.

You've probably been using the same scripts for some time. Many of them may be written using the Bourne shell scripting language or DOS batch files. A problem arises, however, if you need to port your applications to a new platform or if some of the procedures change. Because Perl runs on multiple platforms, it's very effective for hiding platform differences in your scripts. In addition, Perl handles complex tasks much better than the Bourne shell or DOS batch files, making your scripts easier to change and update.

Use the following sections as a source of ideas to find how Perl can best work in your environment.

Sending Email When the Task Completes

If you develop large applications, the typical compile and link build process may take a long time to complete. For example, I'm used to overnight builds. When I arrive in the morning, I'd like a status message that tells me whether or not the build completed. One way to do this is to use Perl to send you an email message. A brief message can describe the cause of the failure or cheer you on if all goes well.

Chapter 6 covered how you can call the UNIX **mail** program using a pipe to launch the mail executable. A more elegant approach is to use the Mail::Send module.

The `Mail::Send` module is located in the **contrib/mail** directory.

To send an email message with this module, you first need to create a new mail object, using a command like the following:

```
$msg = new Mail::Send(
    Subject=>'Build completed',
    To=>'erc');
```

The `Subject=>` specifies the email Subject: line, while the `To=>` parameter includes the email address of the recipient.

Once you have a new mail object, `$msg` in this case, you can create a mail handle, much like a file handle, and use the familiar Perl `print` command to print your email message. When you're done, you need to close the mail handle.

The code to send a simple message follows:

```
#
# Test of Mail::Send
# to send an email
# message when a
# software build completes.
#
use Mail::Send;

# Create header.

$msg = new Mail::Send(
    Subject=>'Build completed',
    To=>'erc@yonsen.com');

$msg->cc('dev_staff@yonsen.com');

# Create message.
```

```
$mail_handle = $msg->open;

print $mail_handle "The software build";
print $mail_handle " has completed successfully.\n";
print $mail_handle "Oh, joy!\n";

# Send message.
$mail_handle->close;


# mailbld.pl
```

The Mail::Send module assumes that you have a UNIX system and tries to use the sendmail command to actually deliver the mail.

WINDOWS

Automatically Rebuilding When the Code Changes

If you're used to C or C++ development, you typically have a number of source files (C or C++) and some form of **Makefile**. The **Makefile** contains a set of rules that describe how to compile the application and what source files depend on what other files. In use for many years, **make** is a very handy tool, mostly because, when a source file changes, **make** recompiles only those modules that are necessary. This is very helpful, because compiling often takes a long time, time you have to wait. The problem is that you have to launch **make** manually, normally after you change some source files.

In a typical multiwindowed environment, you'll edit in one or more windows and then, when you have changed a file, launch **make** in another window. If you're using an integrated environment, such as Microsoft Visual C++ or SunSoft Wrokshop, you still need to initiate the environment to rebuild the application. However, instead of manually restarting **make** (or whatever tool you use), Perl can do the work for you. Armed with the Perl functions described in Chapter 3, you can write a Perl script to examine files in a directory. If any file has been modified later than the last time **make** (or your build command) executed, then, it's time to run the command again.

The stat function, described in Chapter 3, can provide the file's modification time. The glob function can get you a list of all the files in a given directory. Chances are, though, that you're interested in only certain types of files, such as all files with names ending in **.c**. The glob function does a great job of scanning for these file names. (See Chapter 3 for more on these functions.)

With these Perl functions, a Perl script can monitor all the C files and then launch the **make** command when any file changes. To avoid using too many system resources, you can call the sleep function (see Chapter 6) to wait for, say, 5 seconds between scans of the directory. One way to implement this type of monitoring script follows:

```
#
# Checks a directory. If modified,
# that is, if a file inside the
# directory changed, then launches
# a build script.
#
# Usage:
# perl scandir.pl .ext "command" sleep
#
# Where "command" is the command to
# run when a file changes.
#
# For example:
#
# perl scandir.pl .c make 5
#

$extension = $ARGV[0];
$command   = $ARGV[1];

if ($#ARGV > 1) {
    $sleep_time = $ARGV[2];
} else {
    $sleep_time = 5;  # Default 5 seconds.
}

$last_time = 0;
```

```perl
# Loop forever.
while (1) {

    #
    # Check directory.
    #
    $last_changed = &check_directory( $extension );

    #
    # If any files have changed,
    # launch command.
    #
    if ( ($last_changed != $last_time)
      && ($last_time != 0) ) {

        $status = `$command`;

    }

    # Store modification time for next
    # iteration.
    $last_time = $last_changed;

    #
    # Sleep for a while.
    # Adjust this to a higher value
    # for a longer delay between
    # checks.
    #
    sleep $sleep_time;

}

#
# Checks a directory and returns
# latest modified time.
#
# Parameter 0 is the file-name extension,
```

```
# e.g., .cxx.
#
sub check_directory {
    my($extension) = $_[0];
    my(@list);
    my($name);
    my($last_time) = 0;

    # Get file names that match.
    @list = glob("\*$extension");

    foreach $name (@list) {

        ($dev, $inode, $mode, $nlink,
         $uid, $gid, $rdev, $size, $atime,
         $mtime, $ctime, $blksize, $blocks) = stat($name);

        if ($mtime > $last_time) {
            $last_time = $mtime;
        }
    }

    return $last_time;
}


# scandir.pl
```

The **scandir.pl** script takes in a file-name extension, such as *.cxx*, *.c*, or *.pl*; a command to execute, such as **make** or **nmake** and an optional number of seconds to sleep between scans of the directory (which defaults to 5 seconds).

It's very easy for PC clocks to be wildly inaccurate. The PC clock defeated some of my earlier tests of the **scandir.pl** script because some of my files were modified—according to the PC clock—at a date far in the future. If you have problems with **scandir.pl** on Windows, check the dates that the **DIR** command reports for the files in which you are interested and the current clock setting.

If any file gets modified since the last time the command executed, **scandir.pl** launches your command using the back-tick method of `` `$command` ``. This method works on both Windows and UNIX. However, there are some disadvantages to the way the process gets executed. You may want to use the `system` function or some other technique shown in Chapter 6. For example, in using **scandir.pl**, you can have **scandir.pl** monitor all the **.c** files in the current directory and simply execute **make** if any of these files change, using the following command:

```
perl scandir.pl .c make
```

Calling **make** is rather trivial. If you work in a networked environment, then you know that compiling code over network links tends to be a very slow process. You may want to edit files on your local machine and then, when a file changes, copy it to a remote machine on the network and compile there. Or, you may want to compile locally and then copy the newly changed files back to the network host where the files normally reside. In such cases, the command that **scandir.pl** executes gets increasingly complex, making **scandir.pl** much more useful.

The **scandir.pl** script is just one example where Perl can help in your environment.

Using Perl in Your Software Environment

If you're developing software, I hope you use some form of version control software to allow you to re-create older versions of files should anything go wrong. Many things *have* gone wrong for me, so I always try to use such tools. Most sites use freeware tools like RCS (short for revision control system), SCCS (source code control system), or commercial tools like PVCS or ClearCase.

All these tools use different commands to check files in and out and to extract various versions of files. You can use Perl to hide these oft-forgotten commands behind simple names like **check_in** or **check_out**.

On Windows, you should use the **pl2bat.bat** batch file to convert your Perl scripts into DOS batch files, so that you can simply type the file name to execute the script.

Automated Testing

Perl can also help with automated testing in both launching the commands that conduct the tests and parsing the test results. Most code tests result in copious textual output that must somehow be compared against a desired outcome to see if the test passed. If your tests output text files, Perl becomes a great tool for searching for problems encountered in the text.

Scanning for Include Files

C and C++ code uses a lot of include files, which act very much like Perl's use and require statements. Commonly, C or C++ code includes files that include other files, that include other files, and so on. If you need to figure out which files depend on which other files, you need to trace this tree of include files.

To help with this, the C::Scan module comes in handy.

CD-ROM

This module is not part of standard Perl, so you'll need to install it. Look in the **contrib/softdev** directory on the CD-ROM.

The C::Scan module allows you to scan a C code file (this module does not understand C++) for all files included, and all the files these files include, and so on. To do this, you need to provide two things: the name of the C file to check and any defines that get set in your code or passed to the compiler. The most common defines tell C::Scan about nonstandard locations for include files. On Hewlett-Packard systems, for example, the X Window include files reside in **/usr/include/X11R5**, a nonstandard location.

To start using the C::Scan module, you need to begin with the use statement:

```
use C::Scan;
```

Then, you need to create a new Perl object for your C source file, as follows:

```
$c = new C::Scan 'filename' => "filename.c";
```

This allows you to start scanning the given file name. To tell the C::Scan module about the defines you use when compiling, use the set subroutine with syntax like the following:

```
$c->set('Defines' => "-I/usr/include/X11R5");
```

This object-oriented syntax leads to strange Perl statements, like the following code, which extracts a Perl list of all the include files the C file depends on:

```
@inclist = @{$c->get('includes') };
```

After this statement completes, the list @inclist contains all the include files. You can test this with the following code:

```
#
# Use of the C::Scan module
# to generate an include file list.
#
# Usage:
#
#   perl cscan.pl filename "-I/includedirs"
#
use C::Scan;

$filename = $ARGV[0];
$incdirs  = $ARGV[1];

$c = new C::Scan 'filename' => $filename;

if ( $#ARGV >= 1) {
    $c->set('Defines' => $incdirs);
}

#
# Get list of included files.
#
@inclist = @{$c->get('includes') };
```

```
@sorted = sort( @inclist );

foreach $incfile (@sorted) {

    print "$incfile\n";
}

# cscan.pl
```

Generating Documentation with Perl

One of the great problems in documenting code is that the documentation becomes out of date when the code gets updated. This classic problem in software engineering calls for discipline but instead generates lots of finger pointing and not much else. One way to help with this problem is to use Perl or some other tool to generate documentation from the code, usually from specially formatted comments in the code.

Many companies specify that each function, in whatever programming language, begin with a specially formatted header comment block. This comment block describes the function and any algorithms used. In most cases, you're supposed to follow a particular format for these comment blocks (or else you'll get in trouble with your boss).

If your site uses something like this, you can use Perl's string-handling capabilities to extract the function documentation, creating an easier way to look up information about the functions in your source code base. For example, you may want to create a cross-reference, or even a hypertext-linked HTML Web document.

The theory here is that of all the sources of documentation, the code—and the comments in the code—are more likely to be correct than anything else. External documents often become outdated as the code changes. Of course, the comments in the code may also become outdated, but such discrepancies are easier to spot and correct. In addition, any documentation extracted directly from the code—not the comments—is guaranteed to be correct, since it's the actual code. For example, you can go a long way toward documenting C++ libraries by extracting classes definitions and member function signatures.

You can use Perl extensively to help generate documentation from your code. The key is finding the triggers—the formatted comments—to use to start associating a particular comment with a particular function. Once you capture this information, the rest is fairly straightforward. Because your site no doubt uses a different coding standard, you'll need to develop this yourself.

Some techniques shown in the last few chapters may help. Take another look at Chapter 9 on Web pages. The HTML format has become ubiquitous, and browsers are available for just about every platform under the sun. The use of HTML allows an easy means for creating formatted documents with hypertext links. For example, you can link each use of a class or structure as a parameter to a function to the definition of that class or structure. In addition, the **regen.pl** script in Chapter 9 creates a table of contents using a Perl associative array of all the topics. You can use the same techniques to generate a table of contents for function or class definitions. This is very handy in that Perl's arrays can grow without bounds (the actual bounds are the limits of your system's virtual memory, but that is a fairly large bounds). Thus, you can just stuff data onto an array to use it later.

Generating Code with Perl

If you can use Perl to generate documentation from C or C++ code, why can't you use Perl to generate the code? You can, although it's not easy. A common drudgery with C++ classes lies in the requirement to fill out a large set of boilerplate member functions for each new C++ class you create. For example, your site may require that each C++ class provide a Debug() member function that outputs debugging information, a Print() member function that prints data in the class (or an ostream << operator), and ToFile() and FromFile() member functions that write the class data to disk. All these functions are likely to be virtual, and all share the same function signature.

If you face a similar situation, you can use Perl to generate the start of the C++ header file for a new class. The Perl script fills in the parts of the boilerplate that are the same for all classes; you then only have to fill in the new material (as well as the body of the boiler plate functions, of course).

You can build a script that creates the boilerplate part of the C++ class header. Use the **genclass.pl** script as a guide:

```perl
#
# Use of Perl to generate part of
# a C++ class definition. You'll
# need to modify this for your
# site.
#
# Usage:
# perl genclass.pl classname \
#     "parent(s)" "purpose" > outfile
#
#

if ($#ARGV < 2) {

    print "Error: Usage is:\n";
    print "perl genclass.pl classname ";
    print "\"parent(s)\" \"purpose\"\n";

    exit;
}

$classname = $ARGV[0];
$parents   = $ARGV[1];
$purpose   = $ARGV[2];

#
# This implementation of ToFile
# and FromFile requires stdio.h.
#
print "#include <stdio.h>\n\n";

#
# Beginning comment block.
# Fill in as needed.
#
print "//\n";
print "// CLASS\n";
print "//\t $classname\n";
```

```
print "//\n";
print "// DESCRIPTION\n";
print "//\t $purpose\n";
print "//\n";

# Class definition.
print "class $classname : public $parents\n";
print "{\n";
print "public:\n";
print "\n";

# Constructors.
print "\n";
    # Default constructor.
print "\t $classname();\n";
print "\n";


    # Copy constructor.
print "\t $classname($classname& copy);\n";
print "\n";

# Destructor.
print "\t virtual ~$classname();\n";
print "\n";

# Common functions. Add yours here.
print "\t // Prints contents of class.\n";
print "\t virtual Print();\n";
print "\n";
print "\t // Displays debugging info.\n";
print "\t virtual Debug();\n";
print "\n";
print "\t // Saves data to file.\n";
print "\t virtual ToFile(FILE* fp);\n";
print "\n";
print "\t // Reads data from file.\n";
print "\t virtual FromFile(FILE* fp);\n";
print "\n";
```

```
# Rest of class body.
print "protected:\n";
print "\n";
print "private:\n";
print "\n";

print "}; \t // $classname\n";
print "\n";
print "\n";
```

```
# genclass.pl
```

You'll need to modify **genclass.pl** to better fit the C++ classes used at your site.

Using **genclass.pl** is easy. For example, say you want to create a class named `DisplayObject`, derived from a C++ class named `BaseObject`. You could use the following command line to invoke the **genclass.pl** script:

```
perl genclass.pl DisplayObject BaseObject \
  "Base class for display objects" > dispobj.h
```

This creates a C++ header file named **dispobj.h**, as follows:

```
#include <stdio.h>

//
// CLASS
//      DisplayObject
//
// DESCRIPTION
//      Base class for display objects
//
class DisplayObject : public BaseObject
{
public:

    DisplayObject();
```

```
DisplayObject(DisplayObject& copy);

virtual ~DisplayObject();

// Prints contents of class.
virtual Print();

// Displays debugging info.
virtual Debug();

// Saves data to file.
virtual ToFile(FILE* fp);

// Reads data from file.
virtual FromFile(FILE* fp);

protected:

private:

};     // DisplayObject
```

NOTE If your class inherits from more than one base class, simply pass the class names as one parameter, e.g., "Base1, Base2".

Using a script such as **genclass.pl** can cut out much of the drudgery when creating a new C++ class.

Summary

This chapter presents a number of areas where you can use Perl to aid your software development. Most of these areas are in the form of ideas you can use at your site rather than code you can directly place into your applications. Among these useful areas is the `Mail::Send` module, which you can use to send email when a system build completes.

If you use a multiwindowed environment, you can use the **scandir.pl** script to monitor files in a directory. When any of the files change, the **scandir.pl** script will launch a set of commands to recompile your software.

The `C::Scan` module allows you to scan a C code file (this module does not understand C++) for all files included, and all the files these files include, and so on. This helps check for source code dependencies.

You can use a variant of the **genclass.pl** script to generate parts of C++ class definitions in header files. You can use this script to automate creating the boring parts of your C++ classes.

Perl Commands Introduced in This Chapter

```
C::Scan::get
C::Scan::set
Mail::Send
```

## CHAPTER 11

Perl for Client-Server

This chapter covers:

- Networking with Perl
- TCP/IP sockets
- Creating sockets
- Binding sockets to port numbers
- Differences on Windows
- Listening for incoming connections
- Connecting to a server
- Picking up files by FTP

Networking with Perl

Perl contains a number of built-in networking functions that allow you to create client-server networking applications. The Windows version of Perl, however, hasn't kept up and unfortunately does not yet support all the newer convenience functions. It is only a matter of time before we see this support because the Winsock interface allows Windows systems to support the same Internet protocols that Perl uses on UNIX.

Even though Perl seems to support every UNIX system call and communication method ever invented, the most common means for applications to communicate is via network sockets, using Internet protocols. Because your client-server needs are likely to be very specific to your applications, I really can't guess them. So, this chapter provides an overview of Perl's networking commands in a manner you should be able to apply to just about any networking application. This chapter introduces Internet networking and then shows how to create client and server applications using Perl's networking functions. If you're already well versed in TCP/IP sockets, then you can skip ahead to the section entitled "Socket-Based Communication."

Internet Protocols

The Internet protocols come in a hierarchy, as befits a system designed for the military. At the bottom layer lies the physical connection, usually a form of Ethernet networking. Ethernet defines the low-level means of connection—the hardware, electrical current levels, and so on. On top of Ethernet lies the Internet protocol, one of many such protocols you could use over Ethernet wiring.

The Internet protocol (IP) provides for the delivery of packets over a network.

On top of IP lies a number of different protocols for handling the data placed in the packets. The most common of these is called the transmission control protocol (TCP). TCP provides for a full-duplex (two-way communication) byte stream connection. A TCP link acts much like a file in that you can write to it and read from it. TCP is considered reliable in that you can safely assume that your message has been sent unless your script gets an error return from a Perl function. TCP almost always lies on top of IP, making for the common acronym TCP/IP.

Another protocol that sits on top of IP is called the user datagram protocol (UDP). Called a connectionless protocol, UDP, unlike TCP, doesn't maintain state between messages. UDP sends out datagrams that are not guaranteed to arrive, so that UDP is considered to be unreliable. The fact that UDP datagrams don't require a full-blown connection setup makes for a smaller, more compact protocol and better performance. The Network File System (NFS), for example, uses UDP datagrams.

In order to communicate between processes based perhaps on separate machines, you need at least three pieces of information. First, you need to know the unique address of the host you want to communicate with. Second, you need to know the protocol to use in the communication, such as TCP or UDP. Third, you need to know the unique identifier for what process on the host you want to connect to.

This last part is the hardest, especially since UNIX assigns process IDs at run time. The way most systems get around this is to provide for well-known service addresses for commonly used protocols. Typically, this is through the use of a port number instead of a process ID. The port number identifies the type of service desired. Port numbers are used extensively in Internet protocols. For example, the file transfer protocol (FTP) uses a particular port number. A process can connect to this well-known port number (the number is 21, as you can find by looking in the **/etc/services** file on a UNIX system); UNIX handles the task of launching the correct server process when a connection comes in on a given known port number.

For most of your applications, you'll want to use port numbers outside of the range of well-known ports reserved by the operating system. Even so, both processes communicating still need to know the port number to use, or the processes won't connect.

Socket-Based Communications

The basic means for networking in Perl uses a software abstraction called sockets. A *socket* is a connection between two processes, whether both processes compute on the same machine or not. The concept of sockets grew into UNIX from the work at the University of California at Berkeley, famous for the BSD, or Berkeley System Distribution, version of UNIX. A socket is a communication stream that acts a lot like a file. When a socket is properly set up—analogous to opening a file or pipe—you can write to the socket or read from it using the same means you write and read to files. The extra work lies in setting up a socket connection.

To set up socket-based communications, you need to first create a socket with the `socket` function. After that, a server process binds the socket to a port number and listens on the socket. A client process connects to a server using the socket.

To start either a client or server, you need to create a socket using the `socket` function:

```
use Socket;
```

```
socket(FILEHANDLE, $domain, $type, $protocol);
```

The FILEHANDLE acts like the Perl file handles we've used so far. The $domain specifies the protocol family, which basically tells whether you want an Internet socket, PF_INET, or a UNIX domain socket, PF_UNIX, which is useful for communication only on one machine. Other possible values include: PF_802, PF_APPLETALK, PF_CCITT, PF_CHAOS, PF_DATAKIT, PF_DECnet, PF_DLI, PF_ECMA, PF_GOSIP, PF_HYLINK, PF_IMPLINK, PF_INET, PF_LAT, PF_MAX, PF_NBS, PF_NIT, PF_NS, PF_OSI, PF_OSINET, PF_PUP, PF_SNA, PF_UNIX, PF_UNSPEC, and PF_X25.

The $type determines what kind of socket to create. You can use one of the following: SOCK_DGRAM, SOCK_RAW, SOCK_RDM, SOCK_SEQPACKET, or SOCK_STREAM. Of these, the most useful are SOCK_DGRAM for UDP datagrams and SOCK_STREAM for a stream-based socket of the type used in TCP applications.

These values are defined in the Socket module.

WINDOWS

As of this writing, the Windows version of Perl does not support the Socket module. If you are running on Windows, you can set a variable $PF_INET to 2 and $SOCK_STREAM to 1, as shown here:

```
$PF_INET = 2;
$SOCK_STREAM = 1;
```

Then, in your scripts, you need to change all uses of PF_INET to $PF_INET and SOCK_STREAM to $SOCK_STREAM.

The $protocol holds the number of the protocol you want to use. The best way to get this number is to call getprotobyname:

```
$proto = getprotobyname("udp");
$proto = getprotobyname("tcp");
```

The most common type of socket uses TCP. You can create such a socket with the following code:

```
use Socket;

$proto = getprotobyname("tcp");

socket(SOCKET, PF_INET, SOCK_STREAM, $proto);
```

Using the Socket Module

The Socket module, which comes standard with Perl 5.002, takes care of many of the chores of setting up socket-based communication. It includes the definition of the numbers PF_INET, SOCK_STREAM, and so on. If you don't use the Socket module, you'll need to look up the numbers for these values yourself. (Look in **/usr/include/sys/socket.h** or perhaps one of the files that **/usr/include/sys/socket.h** includes.)

Building a Server

After creating the socket with the socket function, the next step is to bind the socket to a particular network address and port number. The syntax is

```
bind(SOCKET, $address);
```

You need to pack the $address with the address type (always the constant PF_INET), the Internet address, and the port number.

NOTE The Internet address is the address of the host you want to communicate with. For server applications, you can use a constant INADDR_ANY to represent any client on any machine, if you want to allow such wide-open connections. This is useful because server processes don't always know in advance what processes are going to connect.

WINDOWS You can use 0,0,0,0 in place of INADDR_ANY.

Internet Addresses

A host's address on the Internet takes the form of four bytes, such as 192.68.41.118. This combined number identifies one machine on a network, be it on the Internet or on a local network.

NOTE

Even though ongoing work aims at extending the number of bytes used in an Internet address, right now we only have four bytes.

You can use the `sockaddr_in` subroutine of the `Socket` module to build up the `$address` value for `bind`, using a form like the following:

```
sockaddr_in($port, $internet_address);
```

The `$port` is the port number to use. You need to pick an open port. The `$internet_address` is the packed `AF_INET` constant and Internet address.

You can get the Internet address for a given host name from the `inet_aton` subroutine:

```
$iaddr = inet_aton($hostname);
```

You need to set `$hostname` to the name of the machine to connect to.

To put this all together, a server application will call `bind` like the following:

```
bind(SOCKET, sockaddr_in($port, INADDR_ANY) );
```

WINDOWS

Without the Socket module, you need to do more work to generate the address value used by bind on Windows.

The following code works on Windows for a server process to call `bind`:

```
$PF_INET = 2;

# Use an arbitrary port number.
$port = 2345;

# Pattern used to pack Internet address.
$pattern = 'S n C4 x8';

# Create an address using 0.0.0.0.
$this_addr = pack($pattern,$PF_INET, $port, 0,0,0,0);
```

```
# Bind socket to port number.
bind(SOCKET, $this_addr)
    || die "Can't bind: $!";
```

The preceding code introduces a new function, `pack`, which you can use
to pack data together into a binary pattern. This is necessary to generate the
data needed for `bind`. (With the Socket module, the `sockaddr_in` subroutine calls `pack` for you.) Check the online documentation for more on
`pack`.

Checking for an Open Port

Server applications need to use an open port number. (Client applications
expect that a server process already has set up the port number.) To find an
open port number, you can use the `getservbyport` function, as follows:

```
$port = 2345;
while (getservbyport($port, "tcp") ) {
    $port++;
}
```

The port number 2345, used as a starting place, is purely arbitrary.

Remember that client and server both need to know the port number. This
can defeat the idea of checking for an open port number.

N O T E

After creating the socket and binding it to a port number, the next step is to
listen for incoming connections on the socket. The way to do that is to call
the `listen` function:

```
listen(SOCKET, $queue);
```

The `$queue` is the number of processes that can get queued up awaiting service. For our simple needs, a value of 1 will suffice.

Once the script has set up to listen on a socket, the next step is to accept
incoming connections with the `accept` function:

```
accept(CLIENT, SERVER);
```

The SERVER is the file handle of the socket created by the call to socket. The CLIENT socket is a newly created file handle that represents the connection to the child process. The accept function creates the CLIENT socket from the SERVER socket already set up. The reason for the separation is to allow the server to keep listening for other client connections, on the SERVER socket and reading and writing to and from the client using the CLIENT socket. One server can service multiple clients by calling accept for each incoming client connection, which generates a new socket for each connection.

After calling accept, you can use print to send data out the socket to the client. You can read from a socket using Perl's file-reading commands, such as $data = <CLIENT>, as described in Chapter 3.

When the process is done with the CLIENT file handle, remember to close it, just as you do with any file handle.

Putting this all together, you can create a very simple server process using the following script as a guide:

```
#
# Example of a Perl TCP server,
# using Socket module.
#
use Socket;

# Use an arbitrary port number.
$port = 2345;

# The protocol is TCP.
$proto = getprotobyname("tcp");

# Create socket.
socket(SERVER, PF_INET, SOCK_STREAM, $proto)
    || die "Can't create socket: $!";

# Bind socket to port number.
bind(SERVER, sockaddr_in($port, INADDR_ANY) )
    || die "Can't bind: $!";
```

```
# Listen for incoming connections.
listen(SERVER,1)
  || die "Can't listen: $!";

print "Server listening on port $port\n";

#
# Loop forever, sending a message
# to each client that connects.
#
for ( ; $paddr = accept(CLIENT,SERVER); close(CLIENT) ) {

    # Send message to client.
    print CLIENT "Hello from server.\n";
}


# server.pl
```

The preceding script simply sends a message (*Hello from server.*) to any client that connects. The entire logic of the connection is handled by the `for` loop that calls `accept` and then `close` on the `CLIENT` file handle when the loop begins again.

A typical server built on this model will fork a new process to handle each client connection. This child process remains around until the connection terminates, and then the child process dies. This is how UNIX handles most networking commands like FTP file transfers.

Because Windows doesn't yet support the `Socket` module, you need to write special code for Windows. The following script, **winserv.pl**, acts the same as **server.pl** for Windows (and also works on UNIX):

```
#
# Example of a Perl TCP server,
# without the Socket module.
#
```

```
$PF_INET = 2;
$SOCK_STREAM = 1;

# Use an arbitrary port number.
$port = 2345;

# Pattern used to pack Internet address.
$pattern = 'S n C4 x8';

# Create an address using 0.0.0.0.
$this_addr = pack($pattern,$PF_INET, $port, 0,0,0,0);

# The protocol is TCP.
$proto = getprotobyname("tcp");

# Create socket.
socket(SERVER, $PF_INET, $SOCK_STREAM, $proto)
    || die "Can't create socket: $!";

# Bind socket to port number.
bind(SERVER, $this_addr)
    || die "Can't bind: $!";

# Listen for incoming connections.
listen(SERVER,1)
    || die "Can't listen: $!";

print "Server listening on port $port\n";

#
# Loop forever, sending a message
# to each client that connects.
#
for ( ; $paddr = accept(CLIENT,SERVER); close(CLIENT) ) {

    # Send message to client.
```

```
    print CLIENT "Hello from server.\n";
}
```

```
# winserv.pl
```

Building a Client

Instead of calling bind, listen, and accept, a client calls connect to connect to a server.

You do have to call bind for a client on Windows. You also need to call connect.

The call to connect takes the following parameters:

```
connect(SOCKET, $internet_address);
```

The $internet_address value again gets built from the Internet address—of the server—and port number to connect to. Again, you can use the inet_aton subroutine to convert a host name to an Internet address and sockaddr_in to combine the port number with the Internet address, as shown here:

```
if ($#ARGV > 0) {
    $host = $ARGV[0];
} else {
    $host = "localhost";
}

# Generate network address of server.
$iaddr = inet_aton($host);
$paddr = sockaddr_in($port, $iaddr);

# Connect to server.
```

```
connect(SOCKET, $paddr)
    || die "Can't connect: $!";
```

The preceding code assumes that the connection is on the local machine unless you pass in a command-line parameter with the name of the host to connect to.

Putting this all together, you can create a client that merely prints messages from the server, using the following code as a guide:

```
#
# Sample TCP client.
#
use Socket;

# Use an arbitrary port number.
$port = 2345;

# The protocol is TCP.
$proto = getprotobyname("tcp");

# Create socket.
socket(SOCKET, PF_INET, SOCK_STREAM, $proto)
    || die "Can't create socket: $!";

#
# The host name to connect to should
# be passed on the command line. If
# not, use "localhost", shorthand for
# the current machine.
#
if ($#ARGV > 0) {
    $host = $ARGV[0];
} else {
    $host = "localhost";
}

# Generate network address of server.
$iaddr = inet_aton($host);
```

```
$paddr = sockaddr_in($port, $iaddr);

# Connect to server.
connect(SOCKET, $paddr)
    || die "Can't connect: $!";

# Print all data coming from the server.
while ($data = <SOCKET>) {
    print $data;
}

close (SOCKET);


# client.pl
```

Note how the client reads from the socket using the $data = <SOCKET> command.

WINDOWS

Again, without the Socket module, you need to write more complicated code. The **client.pl** equivalent for Windows follows (this also works on UNIX):

```
#
# Sample TCP client,
# without the Socket module.
#
$PF_INET = 2;
$SOCK_STREAM = 1;

# Use an arbitrary port number.
$port = 2345;

# Pattern used to pack Internet address.
$pattern = 'S n C4 x8';

#
# Create an address using 0.0.0.0 for here.
```

```
# Note: port number is 0, too.
#
$this_addr = pack($pattern,$PF_INET, 0, 0,0,0,0);

#
# Generate network address of server.
# Perl for Win32 fails to generate network
# address of server, so you must insert
# the IP address or pass it via a command-
# line parameter.
#

$serv_addr = pack($pattern, $PF_INET, $port,
    192,68,41,118);

# The protocol is TCP.
$proto = getprotobyname("tcp");

# Create socket.
socket(SOCKET, $PF_INET, $SOCK_STREAM, $proto)
    || die "Can't create socket: $!";

# Bind socket to port.
bind(SOCKET, $this_addr)
    || die "Can't bind: $!";

# Connect to server.
connect(SOCKET, $serv_addr)
    || die "Can't connect: $!";

# Print all data coming from the server.
while ($data = <SOCKET>) {
    print $data;
}

close (SOCKET);

# wincli.pl
```

Note the call to bind is necessary. Also notice the two Internet addresses generated:

```
$this_addr = pack($pattern,$PF_INET, 0, 0,0,0,0);

$serv_addr = pack($pattern, $PF_INET, $port,
    192,68,41,118);
```

The $this_addr variable just exists for the call to bind and uses a local machine address. The $serv_addr variable specifies the server and includes the server's Internet address and port number. The Internet address of 192, 68, 41, 118 (here specified as a set of four distinct numbers) refers to the actual Internet address of the server. You'll need to insert the address of your server or pass the values via a command-line parameter.

To test both the client and the server, you need to run one script in one window (or on a separate machine) from the other script. On the server side, you'll see output like the following:

```
perl server.pl
Server listening on port 2345
```

On the client side, the **client.pl** script prints out the hello message from the server:

```
perl client.pl yonsen
Hello from server.
```

See the online documentation on any of the Perl functions introduced in this chapter and the **perlipc** topic for more on Perl networking. In addition, most of these Perl networking functions provide a thin Perl layer over the existing C functions of the same name. Any good networking book (see Appendix A for an example) can explain a lot more about TCP/IP sockets.

Perl Modules for Networking

In addition to the Socket module that's a standard part of Perl 5, there are a number of freeware networking modules, most devoted to a particular protocol such as a simple mail transport protocol (SMTP) or the more common file transfer protocol.

The Net-FTP module supports the file transfer protocol, providing subroutines for the most common FTP commands.

WINDOWS

Sadly, this module does not yet run on Windows.

For example, the following commands allow you to pick up a file via FTP:

```perl
#
# Example FTP client.
#
require Net::FTP;

# Connect to a host.
$ftp = Net::FTP->new("ftp.bigserver.com");

# Login.
$ftp->login("anonymous","erc@bigfuncorp.com");

# Change to desired directory.
$ftp->cwd("/pub");

# Change to binary transfer mode.
$ftp->binary;

# Get a file.
$ftp->get("filename.tgz");

# We're done.
$ftp->quit;


# ftp.pl
```

The preceding commands connect to some FTP server on the Internet, such as **ftp.bigserver.com**.

All machine, file, and user names have been changed to protect the innocent.

N O T E

If you're used to the **ftp** program, then you'll see how the subroutines in the Net-FTP module correspond directly with user interactions with the **ftp** program.

The script logs in with a user name of "anonymous", very common for public FTP file servers. The password is normally your email address (again, not a real address in the example). Many public FTP servers keep data for the public in a directory called **pub** (short for public).

The binary transfer mode allows us to pick up a binary (as opposed to text) file, which the get subroutine actually acquires.

See the manual page on **ftp** or the documentation for the Net-FTP module for more information.

The Net-FTP module is not part of standard Perl 5. You can find it on the CD-ROM under the **contrib/internet** directory.

CD-ROM

Summary

Because your client-server needs are likely to be very specific to your applications, I really can't guess them. So this chapter provided an overview of Perl's networking commands in a manner you should be able to apply to just about any networking application.

Perl uses UNIX sockets and Internet protocols for its networking functions.

To create a networking socket, call the socket command. In Perl, a socket is a file handle, and you can use file-related functions, like print, to write data out the file handle.

A server application then needs to call bind to bind a socket to a port number (and an Internet address). The listen function allows a server to listen for incoming connections on a port number, and the accept function creates a new socket file handle for the incoming connection.

On the client side, the connect function connects a socket to a server at a given Internet address and port number.

The Perl 5 Socket module provides a number of handy subroutines for dealing with the Internet's strange addressing scheme.

The next chapter rounds out our discussion of Perl by diving into graphical interfaces with the Perl/Tk extension.

Perl Commands and Modules Introduced in This Chapter

```
accept
connect
getprotobyname
getservbyport
inet_aton
listen
Net::FTP
pack
sockaddr_in
socket
```

Graphical Interfaces with Perl and Tk

This chapter covers:

- The Tk toolkit
- Installing Perl/Tk
- Creating Perl/Tk scripts
- Changing widget attributes
- Placing widgets in a window
- Tk menus
- Scrolled text widgets
- The file dialog
- Binding events to Perl subroutines

Adding Graphical Interfaces to Your Perl Scripts

This chapter introduces the Perl/Tk extension, which melds the Tk toolkit (of Tcl fame) to Perl, allowing you to create graphical applications from your Perl scripts.

If you've ever programmed graphical applications with Motif, Win32, or other large APIs, you'll be impressed by the relatively small, simple API presented by Perl/Tk.

WINDOWS

Unfortunately, the Perl/Tk extension does not yet run on Windows. There is hope, though. Tcl and Tk have been ported to Windows and the Macintosh, so it is only a matter of time before Perl/Tk supports Windows.

This chapter provides a brief overview of one of the best add-on modules for Perl, Perl/Tk. Tk, pronounced *tee-kay*, is a graphical toolkit originally written for use with another scripting language called Tcl, pronounced *tickle*. (See Appendix A for more on Tcl.) As a graphical toolkit, Tk provides the ability to create graphical widgets. A *widget* is an interface item like a menu, a scroll bar, or a text-entry field.

Then, your scripts execute Perl subroutines, in the Tk module, that create the widgets that define your interface. Your interface, for example, may require a menu bar across the top of a main window, as well as text-entry fields so the user can enter data.

Once you create all the widgets, you need to call the Tk::MainLoop subroutine, which handles all input events for the widgets. The Tk::MainLoop subroutine loops forever, waiting for user input. Upon input, Tk::MainLoop dispatches the input to the proper widget. For example, if the user clicks a mouse button over a Radiobutton widget, that Radiobutton widget will get the input. Using such an event loop like Tk::MainLoop is called *event-driven programming*.

Event-Driven Scripts

Perl/Tk scripts are considered event-driven in that, after creating all the widgets, your script essentially goes to sleep. The script wakes up when the user interacts with the widgets, moving the mouse, typing letters, and so on.

It can take a while to get used to the event-driven model. The main concept is that, to perform any work at all, you need to set up callbacks in the various widgets your script creates.

Using Callbacks to Execute Perl Code

The whole point of a user interface is to make your Perl scripts interactive in a friendly, easy-to-learn way. The easy-to-learn part is really something you need to figure out; but the interactive part remains the same for all who work with Perl/Tk.

When the user clicks a mouse button over a button widget, for example, the user expects some action to occur. This could be saving a file to disk, initiating a network connection to another machine, or converting all your documentation to HTML format. The action taken is up to you. You need to specify the action through Perl callbacks.

A *callback* is simply a Perl subroutine that gets called when something happens. You need to specify which subroutine to call, any parameters for that subroutine, and under what circumstances to call the subroutine, for example, when the button gets clicked or when the user presses a **Return** key in a text widget.

You'll see how callbacks work in the section entitled "Scripting with Perl/Tk."

Tk Widgets

Perl/Tk provides a number of different widget types, shown in Table 12.1. You can then create any number of any of these widgets.

Table 12.1 Tk widgets.

Widget	Use
Axis	Canvas widget with coordinate axis display.
Button	Calls subroutine when clicked.
Canvas	Area to draw on.
Checkbutton	On/off toggle button.
ColorEditor	Dialog to pick colors.
Dial	A form of Scale.
Dialog	Subwindow for user interaction.
Entry	Single-line text entry.
FileSelect	File selection dialog.
Frame	Groups widgets and can provide a 3D bevel.

Ghostscript	PostScript-viewing widget.
HList	Hierarchical list widget.
Label	Static text message.
Listbox	Presents a list of items to choose.
Menubutton	Sits on menu bar and displays pull-down menu.
Menu	Pull-down menu.
Message	Multiline static text label.
Radiobutton	On/off toggle button; only one can be on at any time.
Scale	For analog entry of values between a minimum and maximum.
Scrollbar	Allows list boxes or text widgets to scroll.
Table	Lays out widgets in rows and columns.
Text	Multiline text-editing widget.
Toplevel	Top-level window used for dialogs.
WaitBox	Dialog that asks you to wait until something completes.

Installing Perl/Tk

Perl/Tk is not part of the standard Perl distribution; so chances are you don't have Perl/Tk installed on your system.

Perl/Tk resides in the **contrib/gui/tk** directory on the CD-ROM.

CD-ROM

Perl/Tk requires Perl 5.002 or higher, so if you're still using Perl 5.001, you need to upgrade. (Perl 5.002 is also on the CD-ROM that accompanies this book.)

See the **INSTALL** file in the **Perl/Tk** directory for complete instructions on how to compile, link, and install this Perl extension.

NOTE The default installation uses Perl's dynamic loading. If you have problems with this, then you may need to compile and link Perl/Tk statically. If you do this, you'll need to use a different Perl interpreter, called **tkperl**, to run your Perl/Tk scripts. If your system does support Perl's dynamic loading, you can use the traditional Perl interpreter, **perl**. On Linux, for example, I had to compile Perl/Tk for static linking and so had to use the **tkperl** interpreter.

Scripting with Perl/Tk

Perl/Tk follows the newer object-oriented style introduced in Chapter 7. Most subroutines follow the model of $widget->subroutine to invoke the given subroutine on the given widget.

To get a flavor of Perl/Tk's abilities to create graphic interfaces, we can start with a simple push button script, which is shown here:

```
#
# A first Perl/Tk interface.
#
use Tk;

# Create main window.
my $main = new MainWindow;

# Create a push button to exit script.
$button = $main->Button(-text => "Exit",
    -command => sub{exit} );

# Make widget visible.
$button->pack;

# Let perl/Tk handle window events.
MainLoop;

# tk1.pl
```

This script creates a small window with one button as shown in Figure 12.1.

Figure 12.1 The **tk1.pl** script in action.

The first statement in the **tk1.pl** script requires the use of the Tk module. If this doesn't work, you have not properly installed the Perl/Tk extension. The next command creates a main window widget, the top-level window of your application. Inside the main window, the script creates a Button widget using the $main->Button subroutine. The command to execute when the button gets clicked is the (unnamed) subroutine that merely calls the exit function. Thus, when you click on the **Exit** button, the script will end.

The pack subroutine places a widget on the screen inside its parent widget and makes the widget visible. Pack supports a number of options discussed later in the section entitled "Adding More Widgets." Finally, the MainLoop subroutine loops forever, handling and dispatching windowing system events.

In the next sections, I'll delve into each of the concepts shown in the **tk1.pl** script in greater depth.

The Main Window

At the top of the **tk1.pl** script, one of the first commands creates a new MainWindow. All Perl/Tk scripts require a main window, the top-level container for all widgets that appear in, you guessed it, the main window.

All Tk widgets are created in a hierarchy. At the top of the hierarchy sits the main window. Inside the main window, you place whatever widgets you want for your script's interface. In some cases, you'll place widgets inside widgets inside widgets. For example, inside the main window, you're likely to place a menu bar. Inside the menu bar, you'll want to have menu buttons and menus. Inside the menus, you'll often want to create submenus. With Perl/Tk, you can nest widgets within widgets within widgets as many times as you'd like. (Sooner or later, you will run out of memory, but you can nest quite a few widgets before this happens.)

The main window widget is then the parent for any number of child widgets. Inside the main window widget, you can create other widgets, such as Frame widgets, that act as parents themselves. Inside these parent widgets you can place other widgets, including other parent widgets, and so on and so on.

Creating Widgets

The standard way to create a widget is to call a method on the parent in which you want to place the new widget. In the **tk1.pl** script, for example, the following subroutine creates a Button widget inside the main window widget, $main, by calling the Button subroutine from the main window widget, as shown here:

```
$button = $main->Button(-text => "Exit",
    -command => sub{exit} );
```

Remember that the $main->Button() syntax is effectively the same as calling &Button($main).

To create any kind of widget, you call a subroutine on the parent widget. The subroutine's name is the same as the type of widget, as shown in Table 12.1.

With each widget you create, you specify a number of named parameters that control options of the widget. In the Button example, the -text option (the text displayed) gets set to "Exit," and the -command option (the call-back—what to do when clicked on) gets set to the anonymous (unnamed) subroutine that simply calls the exit function to quit the application.

You can set a large number of options for each widget. The online documentation that comes with the Perl/Tk extension lists the options allowed for each type of widget. These options control the attributes of the widget, such as colors and fonts, as well as what to do under certain conditions, like the -command callback shown previously.

You can set a widget's attributes when you create the widget by passing the parameters to the subroutine that creates the widget, i.e., the Button subroutine called previously.

If you don't change a widget's attributes at creation time, you can modify them later.

Changing Widget Attributes

The primary way to change a widget's attributes after creation is through the configure subroutine, supported by all widgets. For example,

```
$widget->configure(-foreground => "black");
```

This subroutine sets the widget's foreground color to black. On UNIX systems, the file **/usr/lib/X11/rgb.txt** lists the color names available on your system. (There are a few more color-naming options; see Appendix A for a list of books on the X Window System.) You can use any of the color names from this file. If you do set a color like unknown color name "redorange" and see an error, then you have picked a color that isn't in the X color file.

Some of the more common options are listed in Table 12.2.

Table 12.2 Tk configuration options.

Option	Use
-activebackground	Sets background color when widget is active and when mouse is in widget and can perform an action.
-activeborderwidth	Sets width of border when widget is active.
-activeforeground	Sets foreground color when widget is active.
-anchor	Tells where to place bitmap or text within widget; one of n, ne, e, se, s, sw, w, nw, or center.
-background	Sets normal background color.
-bg	Sets normal background color.
-bitmap	Sets bit map to error, gray50, gray25, hourglass, info, questhead, question, or warning.
-borderwidth	Sets widget border width.

`-bd`	Sets widget border width.
`-cursor`	Sets cursor shape, see **/usr/include/X11/cursorfont.h** for the list of shapes.
`-disabledforeground`	Sets foreground color used when widget is disabled (unresponsive to input).
`-exportselection`	Set to true to allow for copy and paste between applications.
`-font`	Sets font. Use **xlsfonts** to list available fonts.
`-foreground`	Sets normal foreground color.
`-fg`	Sets normal foreground color.
`-highlightbackground`	Sets highlighted background color.
`-highlightcolor`	Sets color of highlight rectangle.
`-highlightthickness`	Sets thickness of highlight rectangle.
`-image`	Sets widget to display an image.
`-insertbackground`	Sets background color for insertion cursor.
`-insertborderwidth`	Sets width of border around insertion cursor.
`-insertwidth`	Sets width of insertion cursor.
`-jump`	If true, scrolling widgets jump rather than move smoothly.
`-justify`	Set to `left`, `center`, or `right`; controls how lines of text within the widget line up.
`-orient`	Set to horizontal or vertical for scroll bars.
`-padx`	Pads extra space (in pixels) horizontally.
`-pady`	Pads extra space (in pixels) vertically.
`-relief`	Controls 3D border around widget, one of raised, sunken, flat (no relief), ridge, or groove.
`-selectbackground`	Background color for selected items.
`-selectborderwidth`	Controls width of border for selected items.
`-selectforeground`	Foreground color for selected items.
`-text`	Controls text to be displayed.
`-underline`	Specifies index of character to underline, used for menu choices.

There are many options. In general, if you skip an option, Perl/Tk will set it to a good default value. Widgets often inherit values such as colors from their parent widgets. Some options apply only to particular widgets. See the online documentation for more information.

Many of these options control attributes in active state. In Perl/Tk, a widget is active if the mouse is in the window and the widget can perform some action. With the Button widget used so far, the widget can perform an action (when you click a mouse button in the widget), so the widget changes color—becoming active—when you move the mouse into the widget. You can turn many of these active attributes off by setting $Tk::strictMotif to 1, which tells Perl/Tk to use stricter Motif interface guidelines. (These Motif guidelines don't allow for the active colors, for example.)

You can see the configure subroutine in the following example script:

```perl
#
# Changing attributes in a
# perl/Tk interface.
#
use Tk;

$Tk::strictMotif = 1;

# Create main window.
my $main = new MainWindow;

# Create a push button to exit script.
$button1 = $main->Button(-text => "Exit",
    -command => \&exit_button,
    -foreground => "orangered" );

# Make widget visible.
$button1->pack;

# Change some attributes.
$button1->configure(-background => "white" );

# Create a second button.
```

```
$button2 = $main->Button(-text => "Push Me",
    -command => \&change_color,
    -foreground => "black",
    -background => "steelblue");
```

```
# Make widget visible.
$button2->pack;

# Let Perl/Tk handle window events.
MainLoop;

# Subroutine to handle button click.
sub exit_button {

    print "You pushed the button!\n";
    exit;
}

# Changes some attributes on buttons.

sub change_color {
    $button1->configure(-background => "red",
        -foreground => "white");
    $button2->configure(-background => "maroon",
        -foreground => "white",
        -font => "-*-times-bold-r-normal—20-140-*");
}

# tkcolor.pl
```

The **tkcolor.pl** script does a number of things. First, it sets the
`$Tk::strictMotif` variable to 1, disabling some of the non-Motif-compli-
ant extensions in Tk, such as active widget colors.

Then, this script creates two Button widgets. Each widget uses a separate callback subroutine. Note how the subroutine gets specified using the
`\&subroutine_name` syntax. You'll use this syntax frequently with your
Tk widgets.

The change_color callback subroutine calls the configure subroutine on both button widgets, changing colors and using a new font. This should give you an idea of what configure can do.

When you start up the script, you'll see a window as shown in Figure 12.2.

Figure 12.2 The **tkcolor.pl** script at start-up.

If you click on the **Push Me** button, you'll see different colors and a new font, as shown in Figure 12.3.

Figure 12.3 The **tkcolor.pl** script after clicking on **Push Me**.

Making Widgets Appear and Controlling Widget Placement

The pack subroutine places widgets and makes them visible. Using special pack options, you have a great degree of control over where the widget appears and how it gets resized.

Some of the available packing options appear in Table 12.3.

Table 12.3 Options for `pack`.

Option	Usage
`-after=>$widget`	Place this widget after $widget.
`-before=>$widget`	Place this widget before $widget.
`-expand=>1`	Allows widget to expand to fill unused space.
`-expand=>0`	Turns off expansion in filling unused space.
`-fill=>x`	Fills widget out horizontally.
`-fill=>y`	Fills widget out vertically.
`-fill=>both`	Fills widget out both horizontally and vertically.
`-side=>bottom`	Packs widget from bottom.
`-side=>left`	Packs widget from left.
`-side=>right`	Packs widget from right.
`-side=>top`	Packs widget from top.

It takes a while to get used to how the pack algorithm works. The following script, which tries packing from different sides, can help:

```perl
#
# Test pack options.
#
# Usage
#   Perl tkpack.pl side
#
#   Where side is one of left,
#   right, top, or bottom.
#
use Tk;

$side = $ARGV[0];

$Tk::strictMotif = 1;

# Create main window.
```

```perl
my $main = new MainWindow;

# Create a push button to exit script.
$button1 = $main->Button(-text => "Button 1",
    -command => \&exit_button);

# Pack widgets from right.
$button1->pack(-side=>$side);

# Create a second button.
$button2 = $main->Button(-text => "Button 2",
    -command => \&exit_button);

# Make widget visible.
$button2->pack(-side=>$side);

# Create a third button.
$button3 = $main->Button(-text => "Button 3",
    -command => \&exit_button);

# Make widget visible.
$button3->pack(-side=>$side);

# Let Perl/Tk handle window events.
MainLoop;

# Subroutine to handle button click.
sub exit_button {

    print "You pushed the button!\n";
    exit;
}

# tkpack.pl
```

To run the **tkpack.pl** script, you need to pass in a side to pack from, one of left, right, top, or bottom. To get a flavor for how this works, the four options appear in the following four figures.

Figure 12.4 shows the default packing.

Figure 12.4 Perl **pack.pl** left.

Note how the widgets get reversed when packing from the right, as shown in Figure 12.5.

Figure 12.5 Perl **pack.pl** right.

For vertical packing, pack from the top, as shown in Figure 12.6.

Figure 12.6 Perl **pack.pl** top.

To pack vertically in reverse, pack from the bottom, as shown in Figure 12.7.

312

Figure 12.7 Perl **pack.pl** bottom.

That's just the tip of the iceberg with `pack`. Most of the peculiarities of the packing algorithm come out when you add more widgets.

Adding More Widgets

Some of the more common widgets include the Label, Frame, Radiobutton, and Checkbutton widgets, as shown in **tkmore.pl**:

```
#
# Adding more Tk widgets.
#
use Tk;

  # Initialize interface variables.
$quality = "letter";
$both_sides = "single";

# Create main window.
my $main = new MainWindow;

# Create a label widget.
$label = $main->Label(-text => "Print Options");

$label->pack;

# Create a frame to hold radio buttons.
$frame = $main->Frame(-relief=>"groove",
```

```
    -borderwidth=>2);

# Create widgets inside the frame.
# NOTE $frame is the parent.

# Each radio button shares the same variable.
$radio1 = $frame->Radiobutton(-text=>"Draft",
    -variable=>\$quality,
    -value=>"draft");

$radio1->pack(-side=>"top");

$radio2 = $frame->Radiobutton(-text=>"Letter",
    -variable=>\$quality,
    -value=>"letter");

$radio2->pack(-side=>"top");

# Each check button has its own variable.
$check1 = $frame->Checkbutton(-text=>"Both Sides",
        -variable=>\$both_sides,
        -onvalue=>"both",
        -offvalue=>"single");
$check1->pack(-side=>"top");

# Remember to pack the frame, too.
$frame->pack();

# Create a push button to exit script.
$button = $main->Button(-text => "Exit",
    -command => \&exit_button);

$button->pack;

# Let Perl/Tk handle window events.
MainLoop;

# Subroutine to handle button click.
```

```
sub exit_button {

    # Print values of variables.
    if ( $both_sides eq "both") {
        print "Print both sides.\n";
    } else {
        print "Print single-sided.\n";
    }

    print "Print quality = $quality.\n";

    exit;
}

# tkmore.pl
```

The Label widget merely displays a static text message, which is useful for explaining the interface and prompting the user.

The Frame widget allows you to group widgets, either for a natural grouping (visible to the user) or for working with the pack subroutine. The pack subroutine works best at packing a single row or column of widgets. Once you get into more complex layouts, it is generally a good idea to start creating Frame widgets and then packing widgets inside the Frames.

Like the MainWindow, a Frame widget can hold other widgets (see the section entitled "Main Window" for more on this hierarchy of widgets). For best visual results, I normally use a border width of 2 pixels and a relief (3D effect) of groove. You can try the other relief options—raised, sunken, flat, and ridge—to pick the effect you prefer.

N O T E Since the Frame widget is still a widget, you need to pack it. Forgetting to do so is a common problem. If you forget to pack a Frame widget, you won't see any of the widgets within the Frame.

Radiobutton widgets allow you to pick from a set of choices. Only one Radiobutton widget (within a given parent widget) can be on at any time. If you turn another Radiobutton widget on, all other Radiobutton widgets go to off.

The -value option specifies what value to place into the variable when the Radiobutton widget is on.

To tell the state of a Radiobutton widget, you use the variable associated with the Radiobutton.

All Radiobutton widgets within the same parent should share the same variable. You don't have to do this, but you'll make your scripts more confusing if you don't stick to one variable for each set of Radiobutton widgets.

N O T E

Unlike the Radiobutton widgets, Checkbutton widgets should each have their own variables. This is because each Checkbutton widget is independent of all other Checkbutton widgets. Because of this, instead of the -value option, Checkbutton widgets support -onvalue (when the widget is in on state) and -offvalue (when the widget is in off state).

When you run the **tkmore.pl** script, you'll see a window like the one shown in Figure 12.8.

Figure 12.8 Adding more widgets with the **tkmore.pl** script.

Menus and the Menu Bar

In addition to the Radiobutton, Checkbutton, Frame, and Label widgets, most of your applications will require menus and menu buttons.

The online documentation on the Menu and Menubutton widgets appears to be incorrect. You can use the syntax shown here to get working menus and then adapt what the online documentation states into the syntax shown in the **tkmenu.pl** script.

A Menubutton widget sits on a menu bar (which is really a Frame widget) and controls a pull-down menu. You need to associate each menu button with a corresponding menu. The menu button takes care of making the menu appear and disappear as needed.

Creating a menu button is easy. You can use a command like the following:

```
$filebutton = $menubar->Menubutton(-text=>"File",
    -underline => 0);  # F in File
```

The -underline option tells Tk to underline the first character (position 0) in the text, "File". For menus, Tk automatically sets up a keyboard shortcut for **Alt-F**. (This follows both the Motif and Windows user interface style guidelines.)

Once you have a menu button, the next step is to create a menu that is a child of the menu button, as shown here:

```
$filemenu = $filebutton->Menu();
```

Then, you need to associate the menu button with the menu. The following code does this:

```
$filebutton->configure(-menu=>$filemenu);
```

That's the easy part. The hard part is adding menu choices. Menu choices are created by special subroutines on the menu for each type of possible menu choice: cascade, checkbutton, command, radiobutton, and separator.

The command type of menu choice acts as a normal menu choice, executing a subroutine (a "command") when chosen. Cascades are used for submenus, and separators create lines between menu choices.

For example, to create the ubiquitous **Exit** menu choice, you can use Perl commands like the following:

```
$filemenu->command(-label => "Exit",
    -command => \&exit_choice,
    -underline => 1);  # "x" in Exit
```

This command creates a menu choice that executes the `exit_choice` sub-routine when selected. Presumably, the `exit_choice` subroutine exits the application. The text displayed is **Exit** and the *x* in **Exit** will get an underline. Tk automatically sets up *x* as the keyboard shortcut following the Motif and Windows user interface styles. (Thus, combined with the **File** menu button, **Alt-F-x** will exit the program.)

Do not pack menu choices or menus.

N O T E

In a menu choice, the text is set by the `-label` option, instead of the more common `-text` option.

N O T E

You can see some menus in action in **tkmenu.pl**:

```
#
# Pull-down menus in Perl/Tk.
#
use Tk;

# Create main window.
my $main = new MainWindow;

# A menu bar is really a Frame.
$menubar = $main->Frame(-relief=>"raised",
    -borderwidth=>2);

# Menu buttons appear on the menu bar.
$filebutton = $menubar->Menubutton(-text=>"File",
    -underline => 0);  # F in File
```

```perl
# Menus are children of menu buttons.
$filemenu = $filebutton->Menu();

# Associate menu button with menu.
$filebutton->configure(-menu=>$filemenu);

# Create menu choices.
$filemenu->command(-command => \&open_choice,
    -label => "Open...",
    -underline => 0); # 0 in Open

$filemenu->separator;

$filemenu->command(-label => "Exit",
    -command => \&exit_choice,
    -underline => 1);  # "x" in Exit

# Help menu.
$helpbutton = $menubar->Menubutton(-text=>"Help",
    -underline => 0);  # H in Help

$helpmenu = $helpbutton->Menu();

$helpmenu->command(-command => \&about_choice,
    -label => "About TkMenu...",
    -underline => 0); # A in About

$helpbutton->configure(-menu=>$helpmenu);

# Pack most menu buttons from the left.
$filebutton->pack(-side=>"left");

# Help menu should appear on the right.
$helpbutton->pack(-side=>"right");

$menubar->pack(-side=>"top", -fill=>"x");

# Create a label widget for the main area.
```

```perl
$label = $main->Label(-text => "Main Area");

# Set to expand, with padding.
$label->pack(-side=>"top", -expand=>1,
    -padx=>100, -pady=>100);

# Create a status area.
$status = $main->Label(-text=>"Status area",
    -relief=>sunken,
    -borderwidth=>2,
    -anchor=>"w");

$status->pack(-side=>"top", -fill=>"x");

# Let Perl/Tk handle window events.
MainLoop;

# Subroutine to handle button click.
sub exit_choice {

    print "You chose the Exit choice!\n";
    exit;
}

sub open_choice {
    # Fill in status area.
    $status->configure(-text=>"Open file.");

    print "Open file\n";
}

sub about_choice {
    # Fill in status area.
    $status->configure(-text=>"About program.");

    print "About tkmenu.pl\n";
}

# tkmenu.pl
```

When you run this script, you'll see a menu bar and main window like the one shown in Figure 12.9.

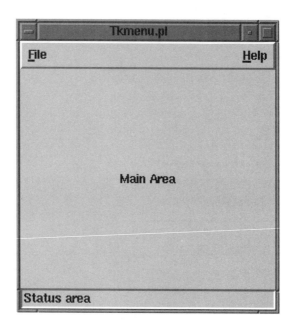

Figure 12.9 Creating menus.

Managing the Status Area

Most modern applications provide some form of status area that alerts the user to what the program is doing. In the **tkmenu.pl** script, a Label widget appears at the bottom of the main window and acts as a status area. At any time, you can place a message in the status area with a command like the following:

```
$status->configure(-text=>"Open file.");
```

(This assumes that you use the $status variable for the status area.)

You can clear the status area by setting the text to an empty string, as shown here:

```
$status->configure(-text=>"");
```

It's a good idea to let the user know what is going on by placing messages into the status area.

NOTE The Perl scripts that come with Perl/Tk show many different methods for creating menus, menu choices and menu buttons. As is typical with Perl, there's more than one way to do a job.

Creating a Scrolled Text Widget

The Text widget provides a multiline text-editing area. To create a Text widget, you can use the Text subroutine. To add a scroll bar to the Text widget, you can create a Scrollbar widget with the Scrollbar subroutine. You then need to associate the Text widget with the Scrollbar widget and the Scrollbar widget with the Text widget. An easier method is to call the Scrolled subroutine, which handles all the associations for you, as shown next:

```
$text = $main->Scrolled('Text',
    -relief => "sunken",
    -borderwidth => 2,
    -setgrid => "true");
```

The preceding command creates a Text widget with a border of 2 pixels and a "sunken" 3D visual effect. The -setgrid option tells the main window to resize only in units of the current font size.

To allow the Text widget to expand to fill up the available space in the main window, you can pack the Text widget using a command like the following:

```
$text->pack(-side=>"top",
    -expand => 1,
    -fill => 'both');
```

You should now be able to enter text into your Text widget. A scroll bar will appear and disappear as needed. (If you don't like this behavior, you need to create separate Text and Scrollbar widgets. See the online documentation for more information.)

Retrieving the Text From the Widget

To retrieve data from the Text widget, you can call the `get` subroutine:

```
$text->get(start, end);
```

The `get` subroutine takes two parameters which indicate where to start getting the text and where to end. Each parameter is required to be in the form of a text index. There are many complicated options for text indices (see the online documentation for more on this), but the simplest form is *line_number.column_number*. For example, 1.0 is a text index starting at line 1 (the beginning) and column 0 (also the beginning).

 Yes, line numbers start counting with 1, and columns start with 0. This is a legacy from the Tcl language.

N O T E

A short-cut index called `end` always indicates the end of the text.

Thus, to retrieve all the text from the Text widget (the most common retrieval operation), use a command like the following:

```
$text->get("1.0", end);
```

To print this out, simply use the `print` function:

```
print $text->get("1.0", end);
```

Inserting Text into the Widget

To insert text, use the `insert` subroutine:

```
$text->insert(start, "text");
```

NOTE

Perl supports multiline text surrounded by double or single quotes, so that you can insert a lot of text at once, as shown here:

```
$text->insert("1.0",    # Line 1, column 0.
    "This is an example of the Perl/Tk
Text widget. You can edit text in place;
configure subroutines for cut, copy, and paste;
and generally work with large amounts of text.
In addition, you can embed widgets anywhere in the
text, for example to view image files. You can
also tag areas of text, changing the fonts, color,
and other visual effects for the tagged areas. You can
bind events to tagged areas, which provides the building blocks for cre-
ating Hypertext windows.");
```

The online documentation describes many more ways to insert text into a text widget.

To delete text from the text widget, you can use the following command:

```
$text->delete("1.0", end);
```

The preceding command deletes all text in the Text widget, by deleting text from index 1.0 (the beginning) to the special index end.

To test out the Text widget, you can use the following script, adapted from the **tkmenu.pl** script:

```
#
# Add a scrolled Text widget.
#
use Tk;

# Create main window.
my $main = new MainWindow;

# A menu bar is really a Frame.
$menubar = $main->Frame(-relief=>"raised",
```

```
    -borderwidth=>2);

# Menu buttons appear on the menu bar.
$filebutton = $menubar->Menubutton(-text=>"File",
    -underline => 0);  # F in File

# Menus are children of menu buttons.
$filemenu = $filebutton->Menu();

# Associate menu button with menu.
$filebutton->configure(-menu=>$filemenu);

# Create menu choices.
$filemenu->command(-command => \&open_choice,
    -label => "Open...",
    -underline => 0); # O in Open

$filemenu->command(-command => \&dump_choice,
    -label => "Dump",
    -underline => 0); # D in Dump

$filemenu->separator;

$filemenu->command(-label => "Exit",
    -command => \&exit_choice,
    -underline => 1);  # "x" in Exit

# Pack most menu buttons from the left.
$filebutton->pack(-side=>"left");

$menubar->pack(-side=>"top", -fill=>"x");

# Create a scrolled Text widget.
$text = $main->Scrolled('Text',
    -relief => "sunken",
    -borderwidth => 2,
    -setgrid => "true");

# Place some text in the Text widget.
$text->insert("1.0",    # Line 1, column 0.
```

```
    "This is an example of the Perl/Tk
Text widget. You can edit text in place;
configure subroutines for cut, copy, and paste;
and generally work with large amounts of text.
In addition, you can embed widgets anywhere in the
text, for example to view image files. You can
also tag areas of text, changing the fonts, color,
and other visual effects for the tagged areas. You can
bind events to tagged areas, which provides the building
blocks for creating Hypertext windows.");

# Set to expand.
$text->pack(-side=>"top",
    -expand => 1,
    -fill => 'both');

# Create a status area.
$status = $main->Label(-text=>"Status area",
    -relief=>sunken,
    -borderwidth=>2,
    -anchor=>"w");

$status->pack(-side=>"top", -fill=>"x");

# Let Perl/Tk handle window events.
MainLoop;

# Subroutine to handle button click.
sub exit_choice {

    print "You chose the Exit choice!\n";
    exit;
}

sub open_choice {
    # Fill in status area.
    $status->configure(-text=>"Open file.");

    print "Open file\n";
}
```

```
#
# Prints out contents of
# Text widget to screen.
#
sub dump_choice {

    # Place message in status area.
    $status->configure(-text=>"Dumping text...");

    print $text->get("1.0", end);
}

# tktext.pl
```

The **tktext.pl** script adds a new menu choice, **Dump**, which prints—or dumps—the contents of the text widget to the screen. When you run this script, you'll see a window like that shown in Figure 12.10.

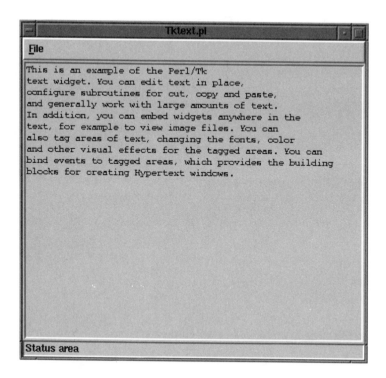

Figure 12.10 The Tk Text widget.

The Text widget remains one of Tk's most complicated widgets. Up to now, you've seen the Text widget as only a multiline text-editing area; however, the Text widget offers much more. You can add tags to control the visual effects of areas of text, and you can embed any Tk widget at any location within the Text widget. When you add the ability of tagged areas to handle events, for example to execute a Perl subroutine on a mouse click, you have the basic framework for creating a hypertext system, such as a Web page viewer. See the online documentation on the Text widget for more on tags and embedded widgets. See the HTML directory for more on Web-based capabilities, including a demo Web browser called **tkweb**.

The text widget can also support cut, copy, and paste operations. See the online documentation on selections and the Clipboard for more information.

Opening Files

Perl/Tk comes with a built-in file dialog, which you can use to ask the user to select a file. (You can also build your own file dialog if you wish.)

Using the built-in file dialog makes it very easy to load up files and save files to different directories. To use a file dialog, you must first create one:

```
use Tk;
use Tk::FileDialog;

# ...

$file_dialog = $main->FileDialog(-Title =>"Open");
```

The FileDialog subroutine creates a file dialog, in this case, with a title of Open.

Creating a file dialog does not make it visible. To make a file dialog visible, use the Show subroutine:

```
$filename = $file_dialog->Show();
```

The Show subroutine returns the name of the file the user selected or an empty string if the user selected nothing or canceled the operation.

You can use the file dialog to load a text file into a Text widget using a
subroutine like the following:

```perl
sub open_choice {
    # Fill in status area.
    $status->configure(-text=>"Open file.");

    # Show file dialog and wait for file name.
    $filename = $file_dialog->Show();

    if ($filename ne "" ) {

        open (FILE, $filename);

        # Clear Text widget.
        $text->delete("1.0", end);

        while ($txt = <FILE>) {
            $text->insert(end, $txt);
        }

        close(FILE);
    }
}
```

You can use this subroutine for an Open menu choice on the File menu. To
show this, try the following script, an add-on to the **tktext.pl** script:

```perl
#
# Scrolled text and file dialog.
#
use Tk;
use Tk::FileDialog;

# Create main window.
my $main = new MainWindow;
```

```perl
# A menu bar is really a frame.
$menubar = $main->Frame(-relief=>"raised",
    -borderwidth=>2);

# Menu buttons appear on the menu bar.
$filebutton = $menubar->Menubutton(-text=>"File",
    -underline => 0);  # F in File

# Menus are children of menu buttons.
$filemenu = $filebutton->Menu();

# Associate menu button with menu.
$filebutton->configure(-menu=>$filemenu);

# Create menu choices.
$filemenu->command(-command => \&open_choice,
    -label => "Open...",
    -underline => 0); # O in Open

$filemenu->command(-command => \&dump_choice,
    -label => "Dump",
    -underline => 0); # D in Dump

$filemenu->separator;

$filemenu->command(-label => "Exit",
    -command => \&exit_choice,
    -underline => 1);  # "x" in Exit

# Pack most menu buttons from the left.
$filebutton->pack(-side=>"left");

$menubar->pack(-side=>"top", -fill=>"x");

# Create a scrolled Text widget.
$text = $main->Scrolled('Text',
```

```perl
    -relief => "sunken",
    -borderwidth => 2,
    -setgrid => "true");

# Set to expand.
$text->pack(-side=>"top",
    -expand => 1,
    -fill => 'both');

# Create a status area.
$status = $main->Label(-text=>"Status area",
    -relief=>sunken,
    -borderwidth=>2,
    -anchor=>"w");

$status->pack(-side=>"top", -fill=>"x");

#
# Create file dialog.
# It will get shown later.
#
$file_dialog = $main->FileDialog(-Title =>"Open");

# Let Perl/Tk handle window events.
MainLoop;

# Subroutine to handle button click.
sub exit_choice {

    print "You chose the Exit choice!\n";
    exit;
}

sub open_choice {
    # Fill in status area.
    $status->configure(-text=>"Open file.");
```

```
    # Show file dialog and wait for file name.
    $filename = $file_dialog->Show();

    if ($filename ne "" ) {
        open (FILE, $filename);

        # Clear Text widget.
        $text->delete("1.0", end);

        while ($txt = <FILE>) {
            $text->insert(end, $txt);
        }

        close(FILE);
    }
}

#
# Prints out contents of
# Text widget to screen.
#
sub dump_choice {

    # Place message in status area.
    $status->configure(-text=>"Dumping text...");

    print $text->get("1.0", end);
}

# tkfile.pl
```

The **tkfile.pl** script, presents the same Text widget as the **tktext.pl** script. But now, you can use the Open choice on the File menu to load a file to edit. As you can see, we're gradually creating a text-editing Perl script.

The file dialog looks like the window show in Figure 12.11.

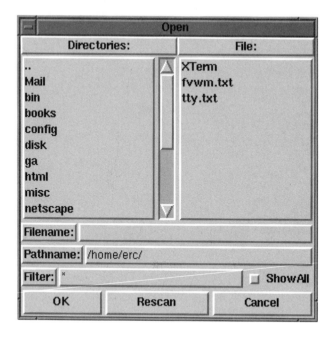

Figure 12.11 The Tk file dialog.

Single-Line Text Entry

In addition to the multiline Text widget, Tk also provides a single-line Entry widget. Most applications use Entry widgets for entering data such as names and addresses.

To create an Entry widget, use the `Entry` subroutine:

```
$entry = $main->Entry();
```

The tricky part for Entry widgets lies in setting up some action when the user enters data and presses the **Return** key.

The Entry widget does not support a `-command` option, so you need to bind the **Return** key or some other event to trigger a callback.

To bind an event to a widget, you need to call the `bind` subroutine:

```
$widget->bind(event, action);
```

You need to encode the desired event in a way that the bind subroutine understands. Normally, this is in the form of <Event>, where *Event* is something like Return for the **Return** key, Delete for the **Delete** key, and so on. The most common event you'll need to bind to a widget is <Return>. (The online documentation shows how to find the complete list of events.)

The <Return> syntax looks a lot like the Perl syntax for reading from a file handle named Return. Don't be fooled.

The action part can be a reference to a subroutine, in the form of \&sub-routine. (There are a number of other forms available, too. See the online documentation on **perlref** for more on this subject.)

So, to bind the **Return** key in our Entry widget, you can use the following command:

```
$entry->bind("<Return>", \&handle_return );
```

The preceding command binds the **Return** key to the handle_return subroutine.

Inside this handle_return subroutine, we'll probably need to retrieve the text from the Entry widget. You can use the get subroutine to do this:

```
$txt = $entry->get();
```

To put this all together, you can create an Entry widget and retrieve the text typed into it with the following script:

```
#
# Using the Entry widget.
#
use Tk;

# Create main window.
```

```perl
my $main = new MainWindow;

$label =
    $main->Label(-text=>"Enter user name:");

$label->pack(-side=>"left");

# Create an Entry widget.
$entry = $main->Entry();

# Bind return key to a subroutine.
$entry->bind("<Return>", \&handle_return );

$entry->pack(-side=>"left");

# Let Perl/Tk handle window events.
MainLoop;

# Subroutine to handle Return key.
sub handle_return {

    $txt = $entry->get();

    print "You entered $txt\n";
    exit;
}

# tkentry.pl
```

When you run this script, you'll see a window like the one in Figure 12.12.

Figure 12.12 The Tk Entry widget.

For More Information on Perl/Tk

This chapter barely touched the surface of all that Perl/Tk offers. In the directories on the CD-ROM under **contrib/gui/tk**, you'll see a plethora of Perl modules (look for names ending in *.pm*) with interesting names. Browse through the code and the demo scripts.

Since the Perl/Tk extension remains under development, the online documentation can be sketchy at best and plain wrong at worst. As you browse the directories, you'll see many sample and demonstration scripts that should guide you as you learn more about this neat extension. In the **contrib/gui/tk** subdirectory, you'll find **UserGuide.pod**. This file contains some good introductory material.

Much of Perl/Tk builds on the original Tcl/Tk. In fact, most of the documentation is merely the Tcl documentation converted to Perl syntax. Furthermore, there's even a sample Perl script, **tcl2perl**, that converts Tcl syntax to Perl. Because of this close connection to Tcl/Tk, you may want to study this connection by reading a book such as *Graphical Applications with Tcl and Tk*. See Appendix A for more information.

The frequently asked questions list on Perl/Tk appears on the Internet at the following location:

```
http://w4.lns.cornell.edu/~pvhp/ptk/ptkFAQ.html
```

You'll also find a general overview and a set of online documentation at the following location:

```
http://w4.lns.cornell.edu/~pvhp/ptk/doc/overview.htm
```

Summary

The Perl/Tk extension melds the Tk toolkit, of Tcl fame, with Perl, allowing you to create graphical interfaces from your Perl scripts. Such event-driven scripts require a slightly different coding style where callback subroutines get invoked by Tk at the appropriate time.

Perl/Tk offers a number of common widgets, such a Menu for menus and Button for a push button. There's a separate subroutine to create each type of widget.

To create a pull-down menu, you need two widgets: a menu button, which sits on the menu bar and handles the task of pulling down the menu, and the menu itself.

You can change the attributes of a widget, such a its text and the font and colors used, by calling the `configure` subroutine.

To make widgets appear, you need to call the `pack` subroutine.

To allow Tk to take over event processing, call the `MainLoop` subroutine.

Perl Commands Introduced in This Chapter

```
bind
Button
Checkbutton
command
configure
delete
Entry
FileDialog
Frame
get
insert
Label
MainLoop
Menu
Menubutton
pack
Radiobutton
Scrolled
separator
Show
Text
```

For More Information

Learning More

Perl is a very large and complex language. As a result, this book necessarily did not cover some parts of the language. By now, though, you should be thoroughly familiar with the basics of Perl so that you can pick up any new feature from the Perl reference manuals.

The first place to look for Perl information is the online documentation that comes with Perl. That's the source for much information and many examples. In addition, it covers the version of Perl you have already installed.

Information on the Internet

In addition to the online documentation, the Internet abounds with Perl information. I've tried to make my Perl Web page a good starting point:

```
http://www.pconline.com/~erc/perl.htm
```

It links to major Perl sites around the world. The main Perl home page resides at

```
http://www.perl.com
```

The home page for the Win32 port of Perl is at

```
http://www.activesite.com
```

Usenet News Groups

In addition to the preceding Web pages, you'll find the following Usenet news groups contain a lot of information about Perl:

```
comp.lang.perl.misc
comp.lang.perl.announce
comp.lang.perl.tk
```

The main newsgroup is `comp.lang.perl.misc.` Virtually all Perl discussions on the Usenet news take place in this group.

Acquiring Updates to Perl

The Comprehensive Perl Archive Network (CPAN) provides a set of linked FTP servers from which you can download Perl sources, modules, and other information. Try the main CPAN Web page at

```
http://www.perl.com/CPAN
```

This page will let you select a CPAN archive site near you.

Books

With the rise in Perl's popularity, a large number of Perl books are available Many of these books address specialized issues like CGI scripting for Web pages.

Other Perl Books

I found these Perl books helpful:

- *Perl 5 Desktop Reference*, Johan Vromans, O'Reilly, 1996. By far the tiniest Perl book, this microscopic text provides a quick reference guide to Perl. It is very useful.

- *Programming Perl*, Larry Wall and Randal Schwartz, O'Reilly, 1991. Dense and forbidding, this book contains a lot of useful information by the creator of Perl, Larry Wall. If you can get beyond the presentation, you'll find this a very useful book. Much of this material comes from the online Perl reference material, but a large section at the end provides a huge number of interesting Perl scripts you can use for ideas and examples. This book covers Perl 4.

- *Learning Perl*, Randal Schwartz, O'Reilly, 1993. This book provides an introduction to Perl 4.

- *Teach Yourself Perl in 21 Days*, David Till, SAMS, 1995. Also covering Perl 4, this massive tome covers just about every feature in Perl 4.

- *Software Engineering with Perl*, Carl Dichter and Mark Pease, Prentice Hall, 1995. Chapter 10's discussion of using Perl with software development tasks barely scratched the surface of what you can use Perl for to aid your software development. This book will give you a number of other ideas.

Web, HTML, and CGI Books

With the explosion of interest in the Internet, you'll find many books on the Web and CGI scripting. Some of the best books include the following.

- *Introduction to CGI/Perl: Getting Started With Web Scripts*, Steven E. Brenner and Edwin Aoki, M&T Books, 1996. This thin book provides a great introduction to Web pages, CGI scripts, and how Perl fits into the picture.

- *Foundations of World Wide Web Programming with HTML and CGI*, Ed Tittel, Mark Gaither, Sebastian Hassinger, and Mik Erwin, IDG Books, 1995. This giant book provides a good background in all things HTML.

UNIX Books

Perl was created on UNIX and adheres to many of the same assumptions that UNIX follows. This convention is great if you use UNIX, but it is tough on

Perl ports to Windows and Macintosh systems. If the concepts of chmod and file permissions are new to you, then you should check out an introduction to UNIX book, such as *Teach Yourself Unix*, third edition, Kevin Reichard and Eric F. Johnson, MIS: Press, 1995.

Other useful books include:

- *UNIX System Administrator's Guide to X*, Eric F. Johnson and Kevin Reichard, M&T Books, 1994. The X Window System is great at providing a common graphical windowing system on UNIX (and other) platforms, but it's difficult to figure out how to configure your environment. This book shows you the where's and how's for configuring X, a very good opportunity for using Perl.

- *UNIX Network Programming*, W. Richard Stevens, Prentice Hall, 1990. By far the best book on programming network applications, this book provides numerous examples of C source code for network tasks. Because most of Perl's networking functions come straight from C system calls on UNIX, this book can provide a lot of the necessary background material.

Windows Books

One of the best places to get information on object linking and embedding (OLE) automation is the documentation and examples that come with Visual Basic. Other good sources include the following:

- *Inside OLE 2*, Kraig Brockschmidt, Microsoft Press, 1994. This book covers much more about OLE than you probably want to know. And, just when you find it out, you'll discover this technology is now part of what is called ActiveX.

- The Win32 reference manuals. If you do much Windows programming, acquire the Microsoft Developer's Network (MSDN).

- *Programming Windows 95*, Charles Petzold, Microsoft Press, 1996. An update of Petzold's classic book on Windows programming, this book is essential if you program on Windows.

For More on Tk

Chapter 12 introduced the Perl/Tk extension. Tk was originally created as the graphical toolkit for another scripting language called Tcl. To find out more on Tk, see *Graphical Applications with Tcl and Tk*, Eric F. Johnson, M&T Books, 1996. The examples are all in Tcl, not Perl, but it's not hard to convert the concepts into Perl/Tk syntax.

Other Sources of Information

I've found the *Perl Journal* to be a very handy publication. You can contact the publishers at the following address:

Perl Journal
P.O. Box 54
Boston, MA, 02101

On the Web, try the Universal Resource Locator (URL):

```
http://work.media.mit.edu/the_perl_journal
```

INDEX